Gardens OF

ECCENTRIC AND EXTRAVAGANT VISIONS

OBSESSION

Gardens OF

ECCENTRIC AND EXTRAVAGANT VISIONS

OBSESSION

GORDON TAYLOR AND GUY COOPER

PHOTOGRAPHY CONSULTANT: CURTICE TAYLOR

WEIDENFELD & NICOLSON

First published in the United Kingdom in 1999 by Weidenfeld & Nicolson

Text copyright © Gordon Taylor and Guy Cooper, 1999
Design and layout copyright © Weidenfeld & Nicolson, 1999

The picture acknowledgements on p.192 constitute an extension to this copyright page

Distributed in the United States of America by Sterling Publishing Co., Inc. 387 Park Avenue South, New York, NY 10016-8810

A CIP catalogue record for this book is available from the British Library

ISBN 0 297 82324 4

Designed by Nigel Soper
Edited by Helena Attlee
Typeset in Spectrum
Printed and bound in Italy

Weidenfeld & Nicolson
Illustrated Division
The Orion Publishing Group
Wellington House
125 Strand
London WC2R 0BB

To Topher Delaney

Contents

LEFT: *An exquisite topiary garden based on the Georges Seurat painting 'La Grande Jatte', Columbus, Ohio.*

INTRODUCTION

She became obsessed with obsession. 'I suppose that is exactly what I was doing in Florida, figuring out how people found order and contentment and sense of purpose in the universe by fixing their sights on one single thing or one belief or one desire'.

SUSAN ORLEAN, *The Orchid Thief*, RANDOM HOUSE, NEW YORK, 1999.

WHAT IS OBSESSION? It is defined in The Penguin Dictionary of Psychology in the following way: 'Any idea that haunts, hovers and constantly invades one's consciousness. Obsessions are seemingly beyond one's "will" and awareness of their inappropriateness is of little or no avail'.

What are Gardens of Obsession? Gardens of Obsession are beautiful, bizarre, camp, cranky, delirious, dreamy, enchanting, eccentric, fantastic, grotesque, infatuated, kinky, kitsch, magical, odd, phantasmagoric, quirky, visionary, whacky, and they are often simply witty!

All of these words can help to define the kaleidoscopic diversity of the gardens shown in this book. They are the metamorphoses of dreams, they are fantasies, ancient myths or allegories made into a physical reality. Each of them represents the realization of one person's innermost, all-consuming desire.

We have interpreted the concept of the obsessive garden in the broadest manner possible. The book contains whole gardens and garden elements of the most extravagant and eccentric type. It encompasses a series of contrasts, with examples ranging from the formal gardens of the sixteenth and seventeenth centuries to the creations of contemporary, self-taught artists.

Gardens of Obsession are usually delightful places, but being both eccentric and extravagant, they can sometimes be repellent, too. Their creators have almost no regard for the locality in which they make these very private demesnes. Indeed, their creations may be the cause of considerable local disturbance, particularly in neighbourhoods which pride themselves upon neatness and the similarity between their front gardens or yards.

Our own obsession with gardens dates from 1974, when we became herb farmers in Somerset. At about this time our great friend Moyra Buchanan Burnett, herself a landscape architect, inspired us to start looking at gardens and landscapes in a more professional manner. Within ten years, we had become garden and landscape designers ourselves. Design had become both our profession and our obsession.

More recently, we were asked by a publisher if we had any ideas for our next book. Our whimsical response to this question was 'Gardens of Obsession', a subject that had been rattling around in the back part of our brain pans for several years. He asked for a proposal immediately.

The vast range of the subject matter made it impossible to shoot all of the pictures for this book ourselves, despite the skilled help of Curtice Taylor, our photographic consultant. Consequently, we began to investigate the collections of photographic libraries. Our enquiries produced a galaxy of images which infinitely expanded our rather sedate concept of the Garden of Obsession.

Photographs poured in from all over the world. There were pictures of many different kinds of gardens. Some were of people obsessed with a single type of plant. Others showed garden spaces

built from 'found' materials such as shells and sea-washed pebbles and stones. In one garden the living rock had been carved into human figures, in another concrete had been cast into primitive human and animal forms.

Gardens of Obsession are so personal that they are unlikely to survive if the creator moves on or dies. The jungle is overtaking Edward James' concrete surrealist garden in Mexico, and the secateurs are even now ceasing to shape a full-size yew locomotive in Gloucestershire. The following pages represent our pilgrimage through the minds and visible desires of some garden obsessives at the end of the second millenium.

ABOVE: *This topiary arch in the Tulcan cemetery, Ecuador, is made from immaculately clipped Arizona cyprus or* Cupressus arizonica. *Architectural patterns have been incised in the thick foliage.*

1 TOPIARY AND GRAFTED TREES

Even the topiary works of the Renaissance, the green ships and helmets,
giants, dragons and centaurs, had something of reason to recommend them,
for by their very strangeness they would be likely to compel attention, to stir
imagination, to strengthen memory, to banish the consciousness of self and
all trivial or obsessing thoughts.

SIR GEORGE SITWELL, *On The Making of Gardens*, 1909.

TOPIARY IS THE ANCIENT CRAFT of clipping and training trees or shrubs to create living sculptures. It has a venerable lineage which stretches from the gardens of the ancient Greeks and Romans to the landscapes of the Disney 'worlds' in twentieth-century California, Florida, France and Japan.

The history of topiary is rooted in the ornamental gardens created around the luxurious villas of the ancient Romans. Like so many of the arts and amenities of civilized living, the impulse to create gardens came to Rome from Greece. Even the Latin word for a gardener, *topiarius*, was derived from the Greek root word *topia*, meaning 'landscapes'. *Topiarii* were gardener slaves of Greek origin who served the Imperial household and other wealthy Roman families. Some garden historians suggest that the *topiarii* may have been slaves taken during campaigns in the eastern Mediterranean and western Asia. In this case they would have brought the

influence of Egyptian and Persian cultures with them. This influence was reflected in the topiary found first in the gardens of Greece and then of Rome.

Pliny the Younger wrote about the topiary in the gardens of his two country villas. He describes 'a terrace, enclosed by a box hedge decorated with various shapes, from which a slope leads between facing pairs of animals cut from box.' His uncle, Pliny the Elder, screened vineyards with cypress, 'but nowadays it is clipped or rounded off to slender outline, and even used in the gardener's art to make representations of hunting scenes, fleets of ships and imitations of real objects.'

From the fall of Rome in the fifth century to beginning of the Renaissance in the fourteenth, topiary in its simplest form of clipped hedges was practised behind the monastery walls of cloister gardens. Records show low, orderly hedges in Val di Ema, the Florentine monastery, and in the northern Italian Certosa di Pavia. The British Museum keeps *The Romance of the Rose*, a wonderful illuminated manuscript dating from the Middle Ages. It shows images of castle courtyard gardens where simple, tiered topiary and shrubs trained on wire frames.

The glorious resurgence of all the arts during the Renaissance in fifteenth and sixteenth-century Italy saw the rebirth of topiary in the grand gardens of the Florentine nobility. In 1459, the great architect Leon Battista Alberti designed Villa Quaracchi outside Florence for Giovanni Ruccellai. Rucellai's diary documents Alberti's designs for the garden and, above all, the topiary and its 'spheres, porticoes, temples, vases, urns, apes, donkeys, oxen, a bear, giants, men and women, warriors, a witch, philosophers, popes and cardinals.'

In the seventeenth century the great gardens of Versailles were built. They became the pattern-book influence on topiary all over Europe for the next century. However, the emphasis was not on the figures and complex architectural structures of the Italian mode, but *charmilles*, or high hedges, which were often planted in beech.

The other popular style was created using low clipped hedges of box, both to edge the principal terrace and to form the parterre at its centre. Clipped geometrical shapes such as cones, spheres and pyramids were cut from yew and box to create vertical punctuation in the design.

The informal landscape, 'landskip', style of William Kent and Lancelot 'Capability' Brown in the eighteenth century meant that topiary was temporarily out of fashion, no longer *à la page*. In the nineteenth century it made a come-back as a necessary garden feature among the *mélange* of earlier architectural styles used to create the grand houses of the high Victorian period.

The Earl of Barrington created one of the most extensive Victorian topiary gardens at Elvaston Castle in Derbyshire between 1840 and 1850. It contained an arbour of topiary birds 4 m (13ft) in circumference and 6m (19 ft) high and a 10 m (33 ft) yew hedge made from plants that were hundreds of years old. Many of the features were brought to the garden when they were already fully formed. John Claudius Loudon wrote the following account of the transportation of the topiary trees to the garden:

Numbers of large plants… had to pass in their journey [to Elvaston Castle] through the town of Derby, and so large were they that the windows on both sides of the street were broken by them.

In the late twentieth century, topiary has become a focus for obsessive gardeners. It is used on a grand scale on sites such as the Ladew Gardens of Maryland or the magnificent Topiary Cemetery in Tulcan, Ecuador. At the other end of the spectrum are the vernacular fantasies to be found in front gardens and yards. These range from large-scale topiary such as boats cut from privet, a steam engine in yew and every kind of green animal, to very small, mop-headed rosemary or box in a terracotta pot, to be found in nurseries and garden centres everywhere.

PREVIOUS PAGE: *The bodies of Tulcan's dead are stacked in beehive tombs enclosed by one of the world's most important collections of topiary.*

LEFT: *Thomas Brayton's topiary garden in Portsmouth, Rhode Island, USA, dates from the end of the nineteenth century. Like all of the topiary in this garden, the elephant is beautifully formed and maintained.*

RIGHT: *The hedges of the Tulcan cemetery are laid out in a formal, rectangular plan. The design includes a series of sharply manicured quadrangles, walks and arcades marked with geometric finials, obelisks, caryatids and animals.*

TOPIARY

THE TOPIARY CEMETERY, TULCAN, ECUADOR. The superb, architectural forms of the Topiary Cemetery, Tulcan, northern Ecuador, represent the pinnacle of the topiarist's art. Almost every guidebook to South America includes at least one photograph of the site, which is about a hundred miles north of the capital city of Quito. Tulcan itself is described by one book as 'a funny, run-down place, a bit Wild West and very sleazy'.

The transformation of the conventional cemetery began only about sixty years ago under the auspices of an agronomist called Azael Franco Guerrero. Once the trees were established, he trained a team of young men to do the obsessive clipping needed to maintain them.

There are three principal types of topiary in the cemetery. Several of the hedges have been clipped to create bas-reliefs of architectural mouldings. Others are deeply incised with portraits of South American and Inca heroes or figures drawn from Aztec, Oriental and Egyptian mythology. Finally, single trees have been clipped into colossal shapes, including one of an elephant and another of an overweight astronaut.

LEFT: *The wonderful condition of the hedges at Tulcan is due to an obsessive regime of maintenance which includes twice-yearly clipping.*

BELOW: *One of the more surprising topiary forms at Tulcan is this gigantic child sucking his thumb.*

ABOVE: *Time has transformed Harvey Ladew's 16 cm (6 in) box plants into a 2.5 m (8 ft) spiral, the perch of the contented, clipped duck seen in this picture.*

LADEW TOPIARY GARDEN, MONKTON, MARYLAND, USA. Boxwood topiary and hedges have been a feature of the formal gardens of grand houses in Virginia and Maryland since the mid-seventeenth century. Over the centuries, unclipped survivors have grown into strange, organic shapes.

Harvey S. Ladew embarked on the almost single-handed creation of this extraordinary topiary garden at Monkton, Maryland, in 1929. It contains a diverse collection of clipped hedges and intricate, evergreen sculptures. Enthusiastic though he was, he can hardly have imagined how dramatic the site would look seventy years on. One man's obsession continues to give pleasure to visitors to this day.

PEARL FRYAR'S TOPIARY GARDEN, BISHOPVILLE, SOUTH CAROLINA, USA. Born in North Carolina, Pearl Fryar moved twelve years ago to Bishopville where he works for the American National Can Corp. Even though he had no previous knowledge of topiary, it was the art of sculpting live plants that fired Fryar's imagination, inspiring him to create these extraordinary forms. The result is a sculpture garden encircling his home, packed with hundreds of trees and shrubs clipped into fantastic shapes.

Fryar's garden has attracted the interest of both the gardening fraternity and the art world. His topiary is in the collection of the State Museum and in the Philip Simmons Garden in Charleston. Efforts are being made to endow a foundation that will maintain and protect the Bishopville garden.

ABOVE: *It is Fryar's long, thin unsupported arch shapes that represent his unique contribution to the ancient art of topiary.*

LEFT: *Box, yew and thuja are the principal plant materials used in Fryar's garden. They are clipped into eccentric shapes, drawn either from Fryar's imagination or from the forms dictated by the plants themselves. Yews are sometimes tied together to form archways and arcades which frame the sun.*

निशाफ GIRAFFE

PHEROZESHAH MEHTA GARDENS, BOMBAY, INDIA. During the time of the British Raj, Bombay, now Mumbai, was known as the Gateway to India, as it was the major port for people entering and leaving the sub-continent. One of the more prominent features that new arrivals would notice was the Malabar Hill rising from the northern promontory of Back Bay. This has been a residential area since the eighteenth century, now it is covered with jerry-built apartments constructed for the *nouveau riche*.

On the main road coming to the Malabar Hill is a Jain temple dedicated to the first Jain, Vijayanara Adinath. This is the site of the Pherozeshah Mehta Gardens, formal hanging gardens which contain some extraordinary topiary animals.

BOXWOOD FLOTILLA, BEER, DEVON, ENGLAND. Ron Russell, a retired coast guard captain, lives in the village of Beer in Devon. In the front garden of the coast guard cottage he has made a flotilla of boats from boxwood topiary.

ZACERO, COSTA RICA. Zacero is in Costa Rica, that beautiful country lying between the Pacific and Atlantic oceans. Near its main plaza is a very ordinary, white-painted church. There is nothing ordinary, however, about the two-acre garden that surrounds it. The path to the church is enclosed by elongated topiary arches. Beyond them are green sculptures of motor cyclists, matadors in a bull ring, elephants and an extensive menagerie of other animals, all bordered by a high, undulating hedge.

LEFT: *The parterre at the Monastero de San Lorenzo is very difficult to maintain. The topiary forms have grown together so closely that they must be clipped from above, using scaffolding.*

MONASTERO DE SAN LORENZO DE TRASSONTO, SANTIAGO DE COMPOSTELA, SPAIN. There has been a garden at the monastery of San Lorenzo de Trassonto since the thirteenth century. In the mid-seventeenth century it was replanted as a complex topiary parterre representing, amongst other things, the griddle on which St Lawrence was grilled. The curator of the local museum believes that the design was taken from that of the medieval griddle used to bake a kind of pastry called *flores*, a Galician delicacy. The cross of Santiago and that of the Calders is also represented.

When the Spanish Church began to disendow its properties, the ownership of the cloister passed to the Duchess of Soma. She and her descendants have kept the box hedges in excellent condition.

BELOW : *All three animals in this English topiary garden look strangely contented. It is as though they realize what pleasure and amusement they give to anyone who sees them, however briefly.*

ANIMAL HEDGES, WORCESTERSHIRE, ENGLAND. There are very few cottages which have a horse and jockey, a lion and an elephant in the front garden. The first two creatures are almost life-size, but the elephant is only a baby. They all sit on top of privet hedges so that they can look over the wall to see and be seen by passers-by. Their owner has spent an enormous amount of time and effort in creating them. They were made mainly for his own pleasure, but they also entrance passing motorists for half a nano-second.

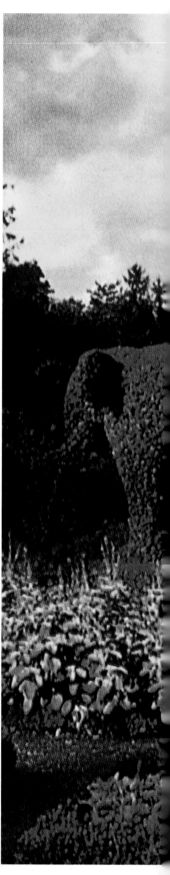

RIGHT: *Brayton's garden menagerie includes a giraffe, a lion, a camel, a unicorn, an elephant, two peacocks and a reindeer.*

GREEN ANIMALS, PORTSMOUTH, RHODE ISLAND, USA. In spite of the very wide variations in the American climate, there has always been an interest in topiary. When the Governor's Palace in Williamsburg, Virginia was being restored in the 1930s, excavation showed that the building had been surrounded by formal box hedging, a holly maze and topiary in various architectural shapes, including cones and spirals.

At the end of the nineteenth century, Thomas Brayton decorated his small country estate with a unique menagerie of topiary animals and birds. This garden makes a welcome change after the stultifying formality of the gardens surrounding the nineteenth-century mansions of the east-coast robber barons in nearby Newport.

BOX BOULDERS, SALING HALL, ESSEX, ENGLAND.
Hugh Johnson has been writing the informative and witty 'Tradescant's Diary' in *The Garden*, the magazine of the Royal Horticultural Society, for many years. In September, 1997 he wrote about the box garden that he and his wife have created.

It all started twenty years ago, when the Johnsons needed to cover the unstable side of the disused gravel pit above their vaguely Japanese-looking pond. Inspired by the trimmed shrubs that they had seen in Kyoto, they planted box. The eighty-eight plants, soon to be added to, are clipped each year by Eric Kirby. He undertakes the task with great caution as the gravel slopes on which the bushes grow have proved to be extremely hazardous. Kirby is the only person who understands the techniques for pruning the box in order to create these slow-growing, ever-changing shapes.

LEFT: Sunday Afternoon on the Island of La Grande Jatte, *George Pierre Seurat, 1886.*

RIGHT: *Mason's topiary replica of Seurat's painting. Most of the figures are made from yew of several different varieties and grown through black-painted steel armatures designed by Mason.*

DEAF SCHOOL TOPIARY PARK, COLUMBUS, OHIO, USA. In 1988, plans were made to turn a rubble-strewn lot in downtown Columbus, Ohio, into an attractive park. James Mason, who teaches sculpture at the park's cultural arts centre, decided to create a variation on Georges Seurat's Impressionist masterpiece *Sunday Afternoon on the Island of La Grande Jatte* . The original painting is held by the Art Institute of Chicago. It is so fragile that it can never be loaned.

The topiary project covers approximately half an acre. The tallest figure is 3.5 m (12 ft) high. There are fifty people topiaries, eight boats, three dogs, a monkey and a cat. The perspective of the topiary layout is exaggerated so that it gives the same effect as the painting. As a result, the foreground figures are larger than those in the background. In Mason's own words:

'Deaf School Topiary Park is a landscape of a painting of a landscape. It makes reference to people in a landscape of activity, to nature and to Western cultural history. Nature has always been a source of inspiration to the artist, and the relationship between art and life is an ongoing concern. Seurat's painting *La Grande Jatte* is a work of art about these concerns... about people (life) in a natural setting (a park or garden). This is a timeless theme in Western art: the Garden of Eden, a yearning for Arcadia. If an artist can paint a picture of a landscape... art mimicking nature then why not a sculptor creating a landscape of a work of art... nature mimicking art? The topiary garden is both a work of art and a work of nature. It plays on the relationships between nature, art and life.'

LEFT: *Here the view of Seurat's garden is reversed. The boats' sails are made from autumn clematis*

RIGHT: *Grasses, creeping thyme and ornamental strawberries are used as ground cover in the Topiary Park.*

**KING RAMA PARK,
BANGKOK, THAILAND.**
The ancient reverence and
love for the elephant, the
splendid 'workhorse' beast of
Thailand and many other
parts of south-east Asia and
India, are shown here in
magnificent clipped form.

LEFT: *Two generations of topiary
elephants graze happily in the King
Rama Park near one of the royal
palaces of Bangkok.*

COMMUNITY TOPIARY GARDEN, LOWER WEST SIDE, NEW YORK CITY, USA. This beautifully maintained topiary grows outside a building on New York's 7th Avenue, between 17th and 18th Streets. It was first created seven years ago when the New York Police Department warned residents that the overgrown shrubs outside their block created a perfect hiding place for rapists. They advised the residents' committee to have the plants removed. One resident decided that this official stance was ridiculous. By creating topiary forms with plenty of stem, he effectively removed the threat of a rapist's bower. The residents' committee was pleased with the improvement to the façade of the building and so were the cops.

THE WHITE GARDEN, SISSINGHURST, KENT, ENGLAND. Harold Nicolson and Vita Sackville-West bought the ruin of a grand Elizabethan manor house in 1931. Over the next ten years they laid out a garden that was to be more influential than they could possibly have imagined. Sissinghurst remains one of the most popular gardens in England, and while every visitor may have a favourite corner or view, the White Garden is perhaps the most famous of all. In fact, the garden and its endless copies have now become almost synonymous with 'ghastly good taste'.

ABOVE: *The enthusiast who originally pruned these shrubs has died of AIDS. An ex-girlfriend now maintains his witty addition to the streetscape of mad Manhattan.*

RIGHT: *Sissinghurst's White Garden is the perfect place for the colour-blind. Visitors can contemplate it from the comfort of a box settee.*

ARLEY HALL, GREAT BUDWORTH, CHESHIRE, ENGLAND. Arley Hall has been owned by the same family for over 500 years; the current owners are the Hon. Michael and Mrs Flower. The garden, which covers 26 hectares (65 acres), is one of the most important in England. It is known especially for having the longest herbaceous borders in the country.

SLEEPING MAN TOPIARY, RAMPISHAM, DORSET, ENGLAND. This piece is reminiscent of the brilliant, sculpted lawn earthworks made during the 1970s by James Pierce in Maine. Pearce was influenced in his turn by the Land Artists of the 1960s, such as Michael

Heizer and Robert Smithson. A bed and a chair have replaced the more traditional topiary frames. Grass, which is becoming ever more common as a material for topiary, has been used to create the fabric covering of the chair seat, the pillow and the blanket.

The man's grassy form was created by covering a model with chicken wire which had been lined with a water-retaining membrane and then covered with earth and sown with grass seed. Once it began to grow, the entire design had to be clipped regularly and fed and watered in the same way as a lawn. We consider the result much more exciting than the endless suburban swards in British front gardens or American front yards.

ABOVE: *A gardener at Arley Hall clipping away at high topiary. In Roman times, his job title would have been* topiarius – *the Latin for gardener.*

RIGHT: *This scene was created by George Wright, the British photographer, in his garden at Rampisham.*

GRAFTING

SIMPLE'S GARDEN, PENNSYLVANIA, USA. Simple's home is at Honeybrook in the depths of western Pennsylvania, where he grows and 'works' all of his own trees. He has turned his camper van into a mobile advertising campaign for his work. The sides are completely covered with painted espalier trees, and in the spaces between the horizontal branches, the different aspects of his craft are listed. He describes himself as 'Simple, the Roving Garden Artist' and he offers to create 'Garden Illusions', 'Topiary', 'Trompe-l'oeil', 'Trelliswork' and 'Façades and Espalier'. The doors of the van are emblazoned with the words 'Specializing in Horticultural Art'.

ABOVE: *Simple relaxes in a fifteen-year-old yew armchair which he has grown without the support of a frame.*

LEFT: *This extraordinary example of the ancient art of grafting is an apple tree. Simple, who can be seen through the heart at the centre of the tree, has grafted five different apple cultivars onto a single specimen.*

RIGHT: *This line of grafted and espaliered pear, plum and apple was also created by Simple.*

LEFT: *Axel Erlandson in one of his many living chairs.*

ABOVE: *The Birdcage Sycamore. The techniques used to create this and the other sculpted trees were approach grafting, bending, often using extremely elaborate wooden forms, and pleaching of trunks and stems.*

BELOW: *In the foreground is the Totem Tree. Behind it is the very first Erlandson grafting triumph: The Four-legged Giant.*

SCOTT'S VALLEY TREE CIRCUS, GILROY, CALIFORNIA, USA. Axel Erlandson, the creator of Scott's Valley Tree Circus, was an obsessive genius. Drawings of the magnificent sculpted trees in his Tree Circus were in Ripley's *Believe-It-or-Not* , an American anthology of the world's weird and wonderful, for eleven consecutive years.

Born in Sweden in 1884, Erlandson emigrated with his family to Minnesota, then in 1902 to Turlock, California. When the family fruit farm failed, he became a land surveyor and also established his own tree nursery. It was then that he noticed the ability of sycamores to naturally self-graft, or 'inosculate'. He began to experiment with other trees such as box, elder, ash leaf maple, loquat, oak, willow, mulberry and acacia.

Erlandson used his discovery to create his wonderful Tree Circus. Trees became his life's work. The results of his work were once described as '…a display of tree culture which beats anything in the gardens of Versailles'. At the age of seventy-seven, Erlandson wrote to the State of California, quoting these words taken from an article published by *Life Magazine* in 1957. He hoped that State might be persuaded to adopt the Tree Circus.

Over a period of fifty years, Erlandson created eighty sculptures, forty of which were still alive at the end of his life. His letter to the State was unsuccessful, but in 1978 Mark Primack, a brilliant young architect, discovered the Tree Circus. He had just graduated from the Architectural Association in London with a thesis entitled 'Botanic Architecture'. Primack led the campaign to save Erlandson's work and it is due to his efforts that the Telephone Booth tree is now safely housed in the permanent collection of the American Visionary Art Museum, Baltimore, Maryland. The trees' ultimate saviour was Michael Bonfante. He planted some sculpted trees at the entrance of the family theme park that he is building at Hecker Pass, California.

LEFT: *Erlandson gave charmingly naïve names to all of his amazing tree sculptures. Among them were Spiral Staircase, Cathedral Window, Lightning Sycamore and Revolving Door. This is the Needle and Thread Ash Tree.*

ABOVE: *The aptly-named Double Heart Willow.*

ABOVE: *Michael Bonfante has taken on the majority of Erlandson's surviving trees. As yet, he has not been able to plant all of them. This is the Double Spectacle Tree, safely box-balled in a giant container.*

RIGHT: *The spectacular Archway Tree.*

2 GARDEN AND 'GREEN' ARCHITECTURE

STERLING. I'll show only his lordship my ruins, and the cascade and the Chinese bridge, and then we'll go into breakfast.
LORD OGLEBY. Ruins, did you say, Mr. Sterling?
STERLING. Ay, ruins, my lord! They are reckoned to be very fine ones too. You would think them ready to tumble on your head. It has just cost me a hundred and fifty pounds to put my ruins in thorough repair. This way, if your lordship pleases.

GEORGE COLEMAN, *The Clandestine Marriage*, (1766)
ACT II, SCENE I

WHETHER THEY ARE BUILT in the classical manner of the eighteenth century or the more modest style of the twentieth, all follies are conceived to give pleasure. Even when they are in a state of rack and ruin, the magic never leaves them.

There are many different kinds of garden folly: belvederes, eye-catchers, gazebos, pyramids, menageries, aviaries and temples. Folly building reached its climax in eighteenth-century England, under the patronage of obsessive, self-aggrandizing landowners.

The earliest, grandest and most influential garden architecture was built by Emperor Hadrian at his villa near Tivoli in Italy. There he replicated on a more domestic scale the buildings that he wanted to remember from his travels: the Temple of Serapis near Alexandria, where his lover, Antinuous, had committed suicide and the Stoa of Poikile in Athens.

Near the ancient garden domain of Hadrian is the Villa d'Este, built in the sixteenth century by Cardinal Ippolito d'Este. Amongst its many grandiose features are the Rometta ('Little Rome'), showing in miniature the Seven Hills of Rome and its major monuments, the Pantheon, the Spetizonium and the Colosseum. Eighteenth-century landowners from all over Europe would have seen Hadrian's Villa and the Villa d'Este when they made their Grand Tour. Afterwards they embellished their gardens and estates with buildings influenced by the 'antique' style. Stone, brick, flint, copper, bronze and even animal bones were used to create the desired effect. Temples of Love, copies of the Pantheon and pyramids of stone or earth were but some of a huge range of follies. They were built both as a gesture to fashion and as a fond reminder to their owners of youthful years spent in Italy.

Garden architecture of the nineteenth and twentieth centuries emerged from more modest socio-economic circumstances. The availability of materials has had much to do with the form of later follies. Latter-day 'eye-catchers' and pavilions make use of materials that are cheaply bought or even free. Concrete, shells, minerals, broken plates, bottles or car headlights can all be incorporated into garden buildings, yards and even houses.

In the context of this book, 'green' architecture refers to buildings screened with climbers, slender fastigiate trees or shrubs. The motive for this style may be a desire to block out the 'here and now' of the world, a preference for filtered light and a greenish haze inside the house, or a simple disenchantment with pruning.

PREVIOUS PAGE: *This twentieth-century folly was built on a grand scale by the late Stanley Norbury in Hampshire.*

FOLLIES

THE PALACE OF WILLOW, AUERSTEDT, GERMANY. A few years ago Marcel Kalberer, an eco-warrior, called together his colleagues in the international eco-network from all over Europe. They gathered in the small village of Auerstedt near Weimar, in what was once East Germany, to plant a living structure made of willow. The Willow Palace is 100 ft (30 m) in diameter and 10 m (30 ft) high. It took the group about three weeks to complete.

RIGHT: *The Willow Palace is built largely from trees that grow next to a stream near the site. Young poplar trees were also planted in bundles to make the uprights or ribs. They were tied into a central post made from a large bundle of young trees.*

ABOVE: *The Menagerie, where the eighteenth-century eye-catcher pavilion was inspired by the wonderful and obsessive symmetry of this late twentieth-century layout.*

THE MENAGERIE, NORTHAMPTONSHIRE, ENGLAND. The Menagerie was the folly or eye-catcher in the park of Horton House. It was designed during the 1750s by Thomas Wright of Durham. The house was saved from total dereliction by Gervase Jackson-Stops who bought it in 1975 and restored it during the 1980s.

The garden was originally created with a central lime *allée*, two hornbeam *allées* and enclosing yew hedges to act as windbreaks. Large circular ponds with jets have been added to the original layout. To either side, two exquisite pavilions have been built. One is circular and classical in style. It is used as an eating-room. The other, which is Gothic and triangular, is used as a guest bedroom. Both are thatched and have walls covered in oak-bole sections. In each case, the façade facing the circular pool is formal. Rustic wooden façades overlook the more informal ponds and plantings. The pavilions are placed in such a way that the porticoes of the two structures reflect and balance each other.

RIGHT: *The classical façade of the eating room, overlooking one of the circular pools at the Menagerie.*

LEFT: *The beaches of the south coast provide the shells that Jack Miles used to clothe the buildings of his miniature village. Local people collect broken china for his mosaics.*

RIGHT: *The Sintra well symbolizes the spiral descent into the netherworld. Galleries and labyrinths are carved into the living rock at each level. The rock is decorated with mystical, iconographic motifs, including the eight-pointed Templar Cross and exquisite acanthus-leaf carvings on the capitals of the fine columns on each level.*

THE SHELL GARDEN, MANITOBA, DOWNTON. WILTSHIRE, ENGLAND. Downton in the heart of Wiltshire is as traditional a small town as you could hope to find in the English countryside. The gardens are tended with the utmost care and usually have all the essential English ingredients: well-mown lawns, herbaceous borders standard roses and wisteria climbing around the front door. The exception is the Shell Garden, laid out by Jack Miles next to his house thirty years ago. It does not contain a single traditional element, and yet it is so well known that coaches full of tourists bound for Bournemouth divert down the main street to see it.

The shell village gets larger every year. At Christmas a local child is chosen to turn on the lights to illuminate all the little buildings. This has become an annual Christmas event, an alternative to the traditional carol service.

NETHERWORLD WELL, VILLA REGALARIA, SINTRA, PORTUGAL. 'Money-Bags' Monteiro was a nineteenth-century Portuguese aristocrat and aesthete. His real name was Antonio Augusto Carvalho-Monteiro dos Milhoes and he was heir to a colossal Brazilian coffee and gem stone fortune. During the 1870s he commissioned a magnificent villa and an allegorical garden on his estate near the Serra mountains outside Sintra. Both the house and the garden were designed by an Italian architect and set designer from La Scala called Manini.

The villa is in a somewhat eclectic *mélange* of styles. The garden is inspired by myth and fantasy. A fabulous nine-level well descends 18 m (60 ft) into a rock promontory on the estate.

LEFT: *The Prince Leopold III's
splendid, English-inspired Temple of
Love at Dessau-Worlitz.*

DESSAU-WORLITZ, GERMANY. Leopold III, Prince Friedrich Franz of Anhalt-Dessau (1740-1817), was besotted by eighteenth-century English landscape and by the enlightened agricultural methods of English landowners. The Prince visited England four times, spending a total of two years in the country between 1763 and 1785. His purpose was to study the landscapes of William Kent and Lancelot 'Capability' Brown at Claremont in Surrey, Castle Howard in Yorkshire and Stourhead in Wiltshire.

Over a period of forty years, Leopold recreated some of the landscapes that he loved on a 25 km (15 mile) area along the banks of the River Elbe. His masterpiece was laid out on 100 hectares (250 acres) of his main estate at Dessau-Worlitz. For his own pleasure and for that of the public he commissioned a Temple of Flora, a Pantheon, a Chinese Bridge and a recreation of the Ermenonville lake and island – the funeral monument to Jean-Jacques Rousseau. It not surprising that the Prince died an impoverished man.

It is extraordinary that these follies should have survived seventy years of Communist rule and enormous cultural change. The prince's *gartenreich*, or garden kingdom, is largely intact. It is being restored with funds given by the Benneton Foundation. Worlitz is visited annually by 1 million visitors.

THE STANLEY NORBURY GARDEN, THE BEECHES, WEYHILL, HAMPSHIRE, ENGLAND. The late Stanley Norbury, a civil servant by day and an obsessive garden maker by night, created his garden piece by self-taught piece; and like Topsy, it just grew. … Norbury said that some of his inspiration came from Spain, Italy and Turkey. These influences are reflected in many elements of the garden, but everything is filtered through his own self-taught sensibilities and obsessive efforts.

Norbury's own description of making the garden is as follows: 'I'd get up at 5 a.m. and work for a couple of hours or more digging, and then in the evening work until midnight by moonlight, and until 3 a.m. once by electric light, summer and winter. It gets you that way, when you get an idea in your head and have a success.'

ABOVE: *Norbury's personalized mélange of styles includes miniaturized Moorish canopies, Italian steps and balustrading and towers reminiscent of Turkish vernacular garden architecture.*

Stanley Norbury did not work to a preconceived plan. As he said himself 'It gradually came like this. I didn't plan it and I had no idea this was going to be the end product.'

LEFT: *This, four-sided, grass pyramid rises 15 m (50 ft) above the water of the lake. It is the burial place of the garden-obsessed Prince and his long-suffering Princess.*

RIGHT: *This aerial view is of the Italian baroque garden in the centre of Portmeirion, Wales.*

BURIAL PYRAMID FOR PRINCE AND PRINCESS PUCKLER-MUSKAU, SCHLOSS BRANITZ, GERMANY. Hermann, Prince Puckler-Muskau (1785-1871), was another German aristocrat of the nineteenth century obsessed by the English landscape style. In 1814 he made a tour of England in order to study its major gardens. During the course of his stay he met Humphrey Repton, and was greatly influenced by his ideas.

After a subsequent tour which took place between 1826 and 1829, the Prince returned to Germany where he extended the Puckler Park at Muskau to 770 hectares (1,925 acres). In 1846 he ran into financial difficulties and retreated to Branitz, a nearby family estate of a more manageable size. There he began laying out an English-style landscape park with a rose garden, a blue garden and a Venus garden in the middle of a lake. The two pyramids were his most spectacular creations. 'Graves are the peaks of far new worlds' were the Prince's dying words.

PORTMEIRION, GWYNEDD, WALES, BRITAIN. Sir Clough Williams-Ellis was a brilliant Welsh architect, planner, conservationist and garden visionary. In 1925 he bought the Aberia estate in North Wales, near to his home at Plas Bron Danw. The existing house was immediately converted into a hotel. Over the next thirty years, the landscape was dotted with an eccentric collection of buildings.

The Portmeirion buildings were made up from reclaimed architectural fragments and bric-à-brac from buildings scheduled for destruction. A double-sided, pillared pavilion was moved from a downwardly-mobile area in Bristol, where it was replaced by a garage for buses. The overall effect lulls visitors momentarily into the conviction that they are somewhere on the Italian Riviera.

The collection of eye-catching structures and Italianate gardens at Portmeirion must have inspired many individuals and organizations to make much greater efforts to preserve historic buildings in the landscapes for which they were designed.

ABOVE: *The follies and the numerous other architectural features at Larchill are being beautifully restored by its owners, Mike and Louisa de las Casas.*

RIGHT: *Arches have been constructed in the four corners of the garden. They are built from antlers shed by elks living in the National Elk Refuge nearby.*

LARCHILL, KILCOCK, COUNTY KILDARE, IRELAND. Larchill is a unique example of an unchanged, early eighteenth-century *ferme ornée* or Arcadian garden. Constructed in 1715, it represents a link between early formal gardens and the more naturalistic landscape park of the late eighteenth century. There are ten eighteenth-century follies at Larchill. One of them is the fortress-in-miniature shown here.

The Lake Folly, complete with battlements, turrets and gun ports, is called Gibraltar. It was thought that the shape of the ground for the fortress was the same as the Rock of Gibraltar.

Mrs Mary Delany, the diarist and botanical artist who was famous for her paper 'mosaicks', visited Larchill in 1778. In a letter to her sister she wrote:

My young godson [later the first Earl of Mornington] is the Governor of the Fort and Lord High Admiral, and has hoisted all his colours for my reception. He was not a little mortified that I declined the compliment of being saluted from the fort and ship.'

ANTLER ARCHWAY, JACKSON HOLE, WYOMING, USA. Eye-catchers and focal points have always been made out of an incredible range of conventional materials. In this Wyoming garden four arches have been made out of elk antlers.

ABOVE: *The sinuous paths at the Garden House create an almost disorientating sense of movement, reminiscent of a drawing by Escher.*

THE GARDEN HOUSE, BUCKLAND MONCHORUM, CORNWALL, ENGLAND. The Garden House was bought by a Mr and Mrs Fortescue in 1945. Mr Fortescue was a retired Eton house master and it is sometimes said that the rarer plants in the garden were grown from cuttings surreptitiously removed from the gardens of former pupils.

Keith and Ros Wiley bought the house after the Fortescues died. They have extended and improved the garden which now contains more than 6,000 species. A narrow area between the tennis court and the bowling green has been transformed into a maze of intertwining, curved paths, creating an amazing optical illusion.

ABOVE: *The focal point of this Dorset garden is a replica of Braemar Castle. The miniature building is surrounded by a moat fed by a tiny river. River water also turns the wheel of a working mill.*

BUNGALOW COURTYARD GARDEN, WIMBORNE, DORSET, ENGLAND. The county of Dorset has the Giant of Cerne Abbas, the spectacular ruins of Corfe Castle and Chesil Beach – all vast in scale. At the other extreme is Mr and Mrs Steele's garden of concrete architectural miniatures.

The late Mr Steele and his wife were Dorset born and bred. They met at the age of fifteen and married at eighteen. They bought their house in 1947 and for the next forty years devoted much of their free time to the creation of the garden.

'GREEN' ARCHITECTURE

BELOW: *Miriam Rothschild herself says that 'the house is ridiculously covered in creepers. I regard it as a tenement. In the ivy I have rats, mice, bats, and an enormous number of birds, including a goldcrest.'*

RIGHT: *Lady Wynne-Jones and her Chelsea town house in full fig for Christmas 1998.*

ASHTON WOLD, PETERBOROUGH, CAMBRIDGESHIRE, ENGLAND. During the nineteenth century the Rothschilds flaunted their wealth and power by building enormous houses surrounded by grandiose gardens. During this period Lionel de Rothschild started the finest collection of rhododendrons and azaleas in Britain at Exbury in Hampshire.

Miriam Rothschild, now aged ninety, has spent most of her life returning the gardens around Ashton Wold, her house near Peterborough, into a natural meadow – a style for which she is renowned. The façade of the house is swathed by the unrestrained and rampant growth of clematis, wisteria, ivy and brambles.

RUSHEEN, LADY WYNNE-JONES, CHELSEA, LONDON, ENGLAND. It was Lady Wynne-Jones' butler who planted the thicket around her house, using willow, apple and cherry trees from her former garden. She has added the climbers and a selection of artificial plants which she changes with the seasons.

Lady Wynne-Jones is obsessed both with plants and with twenty or so small, exotic birds that she has rescued. They live in netted aviaries both inside the house and outside in a foliage bower. She allows that five finches have built nests in a chandelier, but that is their eccentricity, not hers.

It pleases Lady Wynne-Jones to see children coming to look at the façade. 'I believe that emotional stability is dependent on the contact one has with nature as a child. I don't know what I would do without the trees; nature links you closely to deity.' She sees herself as 'an original character', not as an eccentric. She once wrote speeches for Prime Minister Harold Wilson and is a fighter and spokeswoman for heritage and conservation issues in her beloved Chelsea.

WIMPOLE STREET, LONDON. For almost 200 years, Wimpole and Harley Streets in the West End of London have been synonymous with the best and most expensive medical care Britain can offer. The doctor whose practice is run from this house has decided to mask the entire exterior with creepers. This obviates the need for blinds or the equally inevitable swagged, rayon curtains.

OAK SPRING GARDENS, UPPERVILLE, VIRGINIA. Many years ago, some garden designers were improving a small garden in London for a very rich American lady. All the discussion about the design had been at long distance from New York and Palm Beach. When the client arrived she looked at the garden and said, in that east coast, Locust Valley lockjaw twang, '… but I wanted a poor Italian garden, just like Bunny Mellon's'. The professional relationship was swiftly terminated when one of the designers suggested that the client might like some basil plants growing in old coffee cans.

Mrs Paul Mellon is a keen gardener and garden designer. She has created a wonderful garden at Oak Spring over a period of four decades. An arbour of formally pleached crab apple trees links the main house to the library. The flowering plants beneath the trees are changed seasonally.

ABOVE: *Passers-by can almost glimpse the mysterious waiting room of this Wimpole Street doctor's practice, and patients can peek through the tumbling leaves of the façade-encompassing Virginia creeper to life on the street outside.*

RIGHT: *The arbour at Oak Spring requires considerable maintenance. Bunny Mellon may be the only person who could afford such a labour-intensive arbour in her 'poor Italian garden'.*

3 OBSESSED BY FLOWERS

I have not forgot you and have planted many of the early white honeysuckles to gratify your nose when you come to me in the months of April and May... I still have several flowers undecayed... yesterday I severely reprimanded a stock for being unnatural as to bloom in the middle of November and today it is actually closed up. I never knew anything more obedient.

LADY MARY COKE,
to her sister, Lady Stafford (November 1768).

AN OBSESSION WITH FLOWERS can take many forms. It may focus upon one flower or upon any quantity of them. The 12 m (40 ft) floral dog in front of the Guggenheim Museum in Bilbao, Spain, is an example at the extreme end of the scale.

The fashion for ornamental flower-beds dates back to the mid-nineteenth century, when botanical explorers in South Africa and North America brought back plants with exceptionally brightly coloured flowers. Some of the first imports were tender and were nurtured in glass houses. Later in the century, more hardy plant types would be used for massing in infinite variety in the parterres of grand Victorian and Edwardian country houses. Geometric, zoomorphic, emblematic or rococo patterns were all popular.

The Rothschilds displayed an obsession with the carpet bedding style of planting on their estates in Buckinghamshire ('Rothschild-shire') during the late nineteenth century. Weekend guests arriving on a Friday afternoon would see a complex pattern of carpet bedding in the gardens. The next morning they would awake to find that *all* of the plants had been changed during the night, creating a completely different design.

It was at the Rothschild's Halton House that the horizontal bedding scheme became vertical and three dimensional. It was described in the *Gardeners' Chronicle* of 1899 as 'a cushion bed planted to represent a giant ottoman with cords and tassels.' This was the first galvanized-wire floral structure in England.

Three-dimensional sculptural bedding was probably the Victorian horticulturist's alternative to topiary. Municipal park displays then copied this idea and became ornamented with a suite of furniture, staircases, an organ and even a cenotaph, all completely covered in flowering plants. This sort of floriferous obsession never dies. Even now, the combination of red salvias and orange marigolds holds sway in many front gardens or window boxes, and at Chelsea, the most prestigious flower show in the world, there is always some flower-studded horror contributed by a council parks department somewhere in Great Britain.

ARLEY HALL, KNUTSFORD, CHESHIRE, ENGLAND. The garden at Arley Hall is famous for its herbaceous borders. At just over 100 m (300 ft), they are the longest in Great Britain. They were planted in 1846, nearly half a century before William Robinson and Gertrude Jekyll made it fashionable to grow hardy plants.

The borders are backed by yew hedges 3 m (10 ft) high. Yew buttresses at 4.6 m (15 ft) intervals divide the borders into areas, making it easier to alter the co-ordination of the colours. Currently the borders are blue at one end, working through reds to yellow at the other.

KYOTO AND TOKYO, JAPAN. Japanese culture and philosophy is often diametrically opposed to that of Europe. This opposition is supremely evident in gardens and the treatment of plant material. In the West, most gardens and landscapes are intended to be largely 'naturalistic', even if their maintenance is meticulous and time-consuming – as in the herbaceous border. In Japan, everything is so obsessively controlled that a tree or a shrub may be trimmed to exactly the same height for centuries.

Another extreme form of Japanese plant culture is the treatment of an ancient variety of spider chrysanthemum called *saga-giku*, A single plant is turned into a domed form called *ozukuri*. The most important day for displaying these obsessively trained plants is 5 November, the climax of the autumn festival for this national flower of Japan. The chrysanthemum pilgrimage lasts throughout the month, and it is also the traditional time of year for Japanese weddings.

LEFT: *Gardening in this style requires a level of input verging on the obsessive. The Arley Hall border is as magnificent today as it has ever been. The garden owes much to Lady Ashbrook, who has looked after it beautifully over many years.*

RIGHT: *The cascade form of the spider chrysanthemum is called* kengai. *One plant can produce a 'fall' of blossoms 2 m (6.5 ft) long from a single root ball.*

LEFT: *This window box is on the Lloyd Baker Estate, overlooking a square called Percy Circus in north London. It was spied by a passing journalist, mentioned in a local paper, and subsequently awarded a prize for the best window box in the area.*

RIGHT: *A nineteenth-century covey of flower covered birds which delights summer visitors to Mainau.island.*

PERCY CIRCUS, LONDON, ENGLAND. London window boxes are the smallest of city gardens. Some sit jauntily and others forlornly outside windows, while the owner's mood determines what pleasure, if any, they bestow.

People's love for even a few square metres of earth can sometimes have the most unexpected results. It is possible to create a rampant, English country garden in miniature, giving great pleasure any passer-by who happens to look up.

MAINAU ISLAND, BODENSEE, KONSTANZ, GERMANY. Mainau Island was originally the site of a monastery. In the nineteenth century it became the property of the Dukes of Baden. Like so many other nineteenth-century aristocrats, the Grand Duke Freidrich followed the fashion for planting unusual trees and shrubs recently introduced into Europe. Between 1860 and 1880, cedars and Dawn redwoods were planted on Mainau. Italianate terraces were constructed during the same period.

The island was inherited in 1932 by a Swedish nobleman called Count Lennart Bernadotte. He extended the gardens to their present size of 30 hectares (75 acres). The gardens are of interest to botanists and sightseers alike. There is a 'tropical' garden of palms, eucalyptus and bananas which are housed in a large glasshouse each winter. The rose garden has 30,000 plants and spectacular pergolas.

ASHTON WOLD, PETERBOROUGH, CAMBRIDGE, ENGLAND. We first spied Miriam Rothschild at the Chelsea Flower Show during the 1970s where she was introducing the novel idea of growing wild flowers as an alternative to herbaceous borders.

When Rothschild started wild flower gardening in 1970 no one else was doing it. Then, as now, it seemed a wonderful alternative to other, labour-intensive forms of traditional British gardening.

Rothschild collected her wild flower seeds from deserted airfields. She used them to create a collection called 'Farmers's Nightmare'. It consisted of corn daisy, feverfew, cornflower, corn marigold, corncockle and two species of poppy.

Later on, Miriam Rothschild advised the Prince of Wales on his wild flower meadow at Highgrove. It included tulips and camassia in his racing colours.

LEFT: *Miriam Rothschild in her wild flower meadow at Ashton Wold.*

THE TIME TRAIL OF ROSES, WELLS, SOMERSET, ENGLAND. Wells in Somerset is always associated with its amazing thirteenth-century cathedral and Bishop's Palace surrounded by a moat on which swans always glide. This town is the home of Susan Lee, a woman obsessed with the history of roses.

In the half-acre garden behind her house Susan Lee grows more than 1,600 different varieties of rose. She has planted them to form a 'Time Trail', beginning with British natives from before AD 1,000, going through medieval, Tudor, Stuart, Georgian and Victorian types and finishing with the cultivars of the twentieth century.

The names of the roses associated with these eras are Gallicas, Damasks, Albas and Centifolias. Susan Lee's personal chronology starts with the dog rose and ends with 'Smooth Angel' which was developed in 1986 as the first of the the thorn-free roses.

4 RARE PLANTS AND GIANT VEGETABLES

Only four other people in the world have an interest in my plant collection and everyone else hates these plants. Similarly, when I was in Arabia for thirty years, I felt sympathy for the tribes which the other Raj officials disliked. My celandines are exquisitely tiny and have the most wonderful genetic variations.

JOHN CARTER, SOMERSET ENGLAND.

THESE ARE THE WORDS OF one plant obsessive. All of the people that appear in this chapter have focused their attention upon a single genus of plant. Intially they may have taken the plant up as a hobby but gradually their interest has expanded to become an obsession. Many of the people displaying these symptoms have reached retirement age. They are able to devote all of their time and energy to their treasured plants.

We have identified a highly competitive spirit among plant obsessives. They relish the fact that their collections are either unique or very rare. Another common characteristic is their enormous energy. They will go to any lengths to track down and grow the double flower form, the rarer colour, the better conformation of flower and leaf or the largest vegetable or fruit.

RIGHT: *Ganna Walska in 1958, standing proudly with her collection of 'Golden Barrel' cactus and the amazing* Euphorbia ingens *in front of her home in Montecito above Santa Barbara, USA.*

Allied to these features is the compulsion to talk endlessly and enthusiastically about their subject. Indeed they may tell us far more than we ever wanted to know or, as they say in New York, they may 'over-share'. However, their obsessions are certainly of greater interest than many other forms of gardening.

By the ancient Inca ruins of Machu Picchu in the Andes lycastes grow. These are orchids named after a nymph of the air from ancient Greece, or perhaps their name is a Victorian anagram of the word 'calyste' – the Greek for beautiful.

From the majestic *Lycaste longipetala*, an inhabitant of the cloud forests, English orchid growers, using other exotic and fragrant lycastes from Guatemala and Mexico, have bred *Lycaste Hera*. The name was derived from that of the Greek Goddess, daughter of Saturn and queen of Jupiter, King of the Gods.

Dr Henry Oakeley is chairman of the Orchid Committee of the Royal Horticultural Society. He claims to be interested in the beautiful lycaste and anguloa orchids without being obsessive about them. However, he has 25,000 slides, grows almost all known species and one-half of the registered hybrids, raising several thousand seedlings annually. He explores the Andes and has discovered twenty or so new orchids. He exhibits his plants all over the world.

ABOVE: *Dr Henry Oakeley, seen here with his orchid hybrid* Lycaste *'Wyld Elf'.*

LEFT: *This is a specimen plant of the cultivar 'Golden Orb', photographed after winning an Award of Merit and a Certificate of Cultural Commendation from the Royal Horticultural Society in London. This plant is 2 m (6 ½ ft) broad — not a plant for the small greenhouse. It carried seventy flowers over a period of three months.*

WYLD COURT RAIN FOREST, HAMPSTEAD NORREYS, BERKSHIRE, ENGLAND. At Wyld Court three different rain forest climates have been created in the 20,000 square feet of glass house. The staff will give guided tours through the rain forests, not only identifying the massive range of tropical plants but outlining the work of the World Land Trust and its programme to help save tropical forests and other threatened habitats. The Trust now owns and protects over 100,000 hectares (250,000 acres) of forest and wildlife, with projects in Brazil, Ecuador, Costa Rica and the Phillipines.

A visit to Wyld Court is a wonderful experience. One can imagine being in the depths of the Amazon Basin, wandering beneath huge elephant ear plants, while enjoying the scents of the orchids and listening to the chattering of the wildlife.

ABOVE: *Three tropical plant obsessives in a grove of bromeliads. One of them is doing some very close work with moss.*

LEFT: *Roger Grounds peering through a stand of miscanthus in its winter glory at Apple Court.*

APPLE COURT, HORDLE, HAMPSHIRE, ENGLAND. Roger Grounds is Britain's leading expert on ornamental grasses and the author of two books on the subject. He holds the National Collection of Grasses in his Hampshire garden and his wife holds that of daylilies. Neither appreciates the other's obsession!

CARNIVOROUS PLANTS NURSERY, LONDON, ENGLAND. There are genera of plants which have the power to digest animal tissues, absorbing the resulting nourishment and thereby gaining supplies of nitrogen. Carnivorous plants have special means of attracting and capturing the insects upon which they feed. This is done sometimes by viscid glands and sometimes by traps, and sometimes by a combination of both methods. The sundews – like butterworts and the Venus' fly-trap – are the most exciting plants in this family as they actually move to capture their meals.

STAPELY WATER GARDENS, NANTWICH, CHESHIRE, ENGLAND. Barbara and Ray Davies are the owners of Stapeley Water Gardens, one of Europe's leading aquatic nurseries. They also own the Latour-Marliac Water Gardens in the Lot-et-Garonne, an area which Stendhal referred to as 'the Tuscany of France'.

The French nursery is in Temple-sur-Lot, a tiny village of 150 souls. It was founded in the latter half of the nineteenth century by Joseph Bory Latour-Marliac who became obsessed with the beautiful plants of the water-lily family. He devised a manual of hybridization for water-lilies and travelled all over the world collecting specimens.

On his return to France, Latour-Marliac started to cultivate plants in wine casks that he had sawn in half. Later pools were built and he went on to produce about 140 varieties of water-lily, including the first viable, commercial form of the yellow *Nymphaea* 'Marliacea Chromatella'. The nursery was Claude Monet's plant source for the lily pools in his fabled Giverny garden, immortalized in paintings made during the last years of his life.

RIGHT: *Chris Heath is an obsessive grower of carnivorous plants. He belongs to a group of growers that exhibits at the Chelsea Flower Show each year. Here he is surrounded by part of his precious collection of Venus' fly-traps.*

BELOW: *Plant obsessives will go to any lengths to be near the object of their* idée fixe. *Here is Ray Davies, up to his hips in water with specimens from the National Collection of Water-lilies at Burnaby Hall Gardens in Yorkshire.*

LOTUSLAND, MONTECITO, CALIFORNIA, USA. Ganna Walska (1888-1984) was an extraordinary Polish beauty and sometime opera singer, the toast of the court of the last tsar. She is best summed up by her niece, Hania Tallmadge: 'My aunt was famous for many things. Famous for her jewellery. Famous for her costumes. Famous for her great beauty. Famous for her husbands. And now famous for her garden.'

Walska's clothes and opera costumes were designed by great couturiers such as Erté and Callot. Her entire wardrobe, which included a collection of antique clothes, was given to the Los Angeles Museum of Art. She was married six times, twice to American tycoons. Lotusland was Walska's creation and from the outset in 1941, she always cast herself in the role of head gardener. Even in her nineties, aided by two sticks, she would tour the 15 hectare (37 acre) estate twice a day. The garden is divided into separate areas planted with ferns, bromeliads, cycads, cacti and dracaena. There is also a Japanese garden, a blue garden, a zodiac garden, a plant clock and a theatre.

In the 1970s, Walska sold off almost a million dollars' worth of her fabulous jewels in order to create her Cycad Garden. Planted with 500 rare specimens, it is now the world's second most important collection. (Photograph by Robert Glenn Ketchum)

LEFT : *The Abalone Shell Pool at Lotusland is a splendid example of Walska's visual artistry. It has islands made from tufa and fountains crafted from giant clam shells.*

RIGHT: *Madame Walska with her beloved Agave, a bust of herself and her very OK pearls which, as Virginia Woolf put it in* Orlando, *glow 'like the giant eggs of some vast moon spider.'*

LANGLEY BOXWOOD NURSERY, RAKE, HAMPSHIRE, ENGLAND. The nursery is not at all easy to find: cross over a dual carriageway, find an unmarked, pot-holed track through brackeny woods and head towards the remains of the grounds of a Victorian estate. Finally, after some bone-shattering minutes, there is a small, indistinct sign which reads 'To Nursery'. It is well worth the journey. Elizabeth Braimbridge and her retired surgeon husband have the finest box nursery in Great Britain. Little box, big box, shaped topiary box, box yet to be trimmed, box in pots, box lined out, box with signs saying 'not to be touched', box with signs saying 'not to be sold'.

The Lady of the Box is extremely helpful and she can usually resolve a visitor's uncertainties. Most cars depart full of plants that will become tough, evergreen garden embellishments. The Braimbridges supplied the vast quantity of box hedging for the superb reconstruction of the Privy Garden at Hampton Court.

KYOTO AND TOKYO, JAPAN. *Koten engei*, the cultivation of the cymbidium orchid, is an obsession in Japan. The fashion for cymbidiums first emerged in thirteenth-century Heian. During the seventeenth century the Shogunate courts in Edo (Tokyo) brought *koten engei* and the other Samurai class arts to their highest degree of development.

Barry Yinger, a Pennsylvania-based horticulturist, is a leading authority on the cultivation of this plant, having travelled to Japan many times. The Asarum genus (wild ginger) is one of the main types on which competing growers focus. Carefully nurtured specimens are chosen from thousands of seedlings. The prize winners can be valued at $250,000. while an 'also-ran' will fetch only $2.50 per pot.

ABOVE: *When a cymbidium is judged, the conformation of the leaf in relation to the stem, the way in which the leaf lobes meet or overlap, the shape and colour of the leaves and the height and width of the plant are all assessed within strict guidelines on rarity and beauty.*

BELOW : Ken Dade, a prize-winner at the Bath and West Show, Somerset in 1998, shows off the pumpkin in his back garden.

BELOW RIGHT: Ian Neale won the world record for the heaviest beetroot; it weighed in at 18.3 k (40 lb)

THE BATH AND WEST SHOW, SOMERSET, ENGLAND. In the world of horticulture there are some truly eccentric byways. One of them is taken by gardeners obsessed with growing large vegetables. Each grower tends to choose three or four types on which to practice his skill at turning foodstuff into gigantic and probably tasteless objects.

There are a couple of competitive shows at which these enthusiasts may display their talents each autumn. Ian Neale, the winner of many prizes, says that the secret of his success is no secret. It is simply a matter of finding the best seed, water and fertilizer and combining it with nurture and good luck. By monitoring the plants from a succession of seeds and then selecting and saving seed over four generations, he has established the genealogy for his prize winner.

Many prize-winning vegetable growers live in the north of England, where the competition is strong and sometimes downright vicious. Rivals, or their 'assignees', work in gangs. Armed with baseball bats, they will sometimes vandalize plants the week before a show. They also try to make secret analyses of soil, compost and manure in order to discover the winning combinations. The poisoning of fertilizer is not beyond the pale and precious seeds have sometimes been filched or destroyed. All these surreptitious actions are in part the result of vanity and an obsessive competitive spirit, and in part a response to the size of the prize money, which can be as high as £10,000.

*LEFT: Mrs Goddard
triumphant with her gourds.*

*BELOW: Mrs. Goddard won
first prizes with these gourds
in the giant vegetable class
of the Bath and West Show,
Somerset in 1998.*

GIANT GOURDS, HERON HOUSE, SOMERSET, ENGLAND. Tricia Goddard began by cultivating ornamental gourds. This kind of gourd is fast and easy to grow, but it decays quite rapidly. Now she is interested only in hard-shell varieties of gourd. She is particularly fascinated by the varieties that were used by ancient cultures, when they were admired for their shapes and colours as well as their practical uses.

Mrs Goddard collects her seeds locally and in the USA, France and Majorca. She has been growing gourds for long enough to have won many prizes in the gourd class of the major giant-vegetable shows. The largest gourd that she has ever grown was 1.7 m (5½ ft) long. Such a gourd increases at a rate of 7 cm (3 in) a day during the height of the growing season.

In India, Africa and South America gourds are used for bottles, small storage containers, spoons and other utensils. In medieval Europe, long before the invention of flasks and disposable bottles, the pilgrims to Canterbury, Compostela, Rome or Jerusalem would carry their water in these amazing, watertight, dried vegetables.

5 SCULPTURE

… the ancient Romans were excessively prodigal, sparing no cost, to adorn their avenues with curious figures [statues]… Which vanity (although one of the most excusable) is descended on the Italians, whose gardens are the mirrors of the World, as well as for those ornaments as for the excellency of the Plants that are propagated in them.

JOHN WORLIDGE, *Systema Horti-Culturae: or The Art of Gardening* (1677)

GARDEN HISTORIANS SUGGEST that garden sculpture found its way into the culture of western European through the religious practices of ancient Greece. In its earliest form, the cult of Dionysus was devoted to the protection of trees and an image of the god was made in wood. Dionysius, pleased by the mystic rites of his followers, was said to have made them the gift of wine. After this, his image, along with those of Pan and Silenus, was carved in stone and wreathed in ivy, grapes and vine leaves.

Many Roman statues came originally from the workshops at Aphrodisias, not far from present-day Izmir (Smyrna) in Turkey. The excavation of Pompeii revealed an extensive use of garden statuary in the grander houses of the town. Statues were arranged around colonnades and used as focal points at the centre of courtyard gardens where they served both a decorative and a religious purpose.

The popes, cardinals and aristocrats of both sixteenth and seventeenth-century Italy became obsessional collectors of statues which they used to adorn the gardens of their villas and palaces. Their collections encompassed commissioned statuary and the statues of ancient Greece and Rome. A craze for the antique meant that many statues were removed from Hadrian's Villa at Tivoli, the Forum and the former cities of the Roman Empire in North Africa and western Asia.

The fashion for statuary soon caught on in other European countries. Lord Lumley imported statues from Italy during the 1560s for his gardens at the palace of Nonsuch. He collected statues of Diana, the goddess of virtue, as an elaborate compliment to Queen Elizabeth I. Nearly 200 years later, statues were still being imported. Lord Burlington brought several from Italy for Chiswick House in London.

Garden statues found favour once again during the nineteenth century. The growth of the middle class in Europe and the United States led to the mass production of all garden ornaments in cast iron and artificial stone to furnish formal gardens.

Diversity is the key word to describe the garden sculpture and sculptural ornament of the twentieth century. Everything, from the antique to the most modern and eccentric, is available in real and reconstituted materials. The examples in this chapter range from statues of Diana to garden gnomes.

GARDEN COURTYARD, AMSTERDAM, HOLLAND. Pieter Brattinga is a well-known Dutch designer and a professor of art. During the late 1950s, he lived in America. It is hard to say whether it was Dutch thriftiness or a sudden flurry of American-style concern for the environment that led him to recycle all the wooden crates in which he had brought back his books from America. The same crates are neatly placed against one wall of his small courtyard garden. They are now used to store stacks of wood for his fire. In the middle of the firewood is a life-size plaster copy of the *Venus de Milo*. Fashions in art education in the 1960s and '70s dispensed with classical or even live models. Being found surplus to requirements, this Venus was thrown onto a junk heap, from which Brattinga rescued her.

ABOVE: *A statue of the* Venus de Milo *standing between shards of North American timber in a Dutch designer's garden.*

GARDEN SHRINE OF FERTILITY, BANGKOK, THAILAND. Thai ladies have always used many different rites to either establish or increase their fertility. One such is this garden shrine in the middle of Bangkok, replete with offerings of stone and wooden phalluses ranging from 1 to 2 m (3½ to 6½ ft) in length. Other offerings include jasmine wreaths, candles and sticks of incense.

Women who visit the shrine pray both for children – male – and also for mundane matters such as winning the national lottery, getting a better job, passing an examination or making a profit in business.

Some years ago a Hilton Hotel was built immediately adjacent to this shrine garden. The building had to be planned with an entrance facing away from the shrine. In this way, the sensibilities of the mainly Western, Christian guests could be protected – until they stumbled on Bangkok's notoriously wild sex clubs.

ABOVE: *This fertitlity shrine honours the ancient Thai spirit, Chao Mae Tuptim. The word* tuptim *means both 'pomegranate' and 'ruby' in the Thai language.*

LEFT: *César's thumb standing in the garden of the Galerie Beaubourg in Vence, Paris' main artistic outpost in the south of France.*

GALERIE BEAUBOURG, VENCE, FRANCE. This giant stone thumb is by César, an artist of the Neo-Realist school who died in 1998. The group included other, equally avant-garde members like Yves Klein, Jean Tinguely and Niki de Saint-Phalle.

César became France's best known contemporary sculptor. Two images sum up his distinctive appeal. One is a wall or tower of crushed cars and the other is the giant, upright thumb. César's famous thumb has been endlessly reproduced in plastic, metal and glass. There is even a convenient desk-top paperweight in life size.

FINCHLEY, NORTH LONDON, ENGLAND. We assume that the headless house-husband in this London garden has just done the family wash, while his power-suited, brief-case-carrying wife climbs the corporate ladder.

ABOVE: *An eccentric fibreglass sculpture which was body-moulded from life by Judy Wiseman. The figure stands by an amusing eco-friendly, grass-roofed garden shed in a north-London garden.*

RIGHT: *Perhaps the most surprising thing of all in the park of the Villa Voltalarca, Italy, is this statue of a man startled while attending to a call of nature.*

VILLA VOLTARCA, LE MARCHE, ITALY. Villa Voltalarca is a large, nineteenth-century estate in Le Marche, on Italy's east coast. The villa dates from 1727 and in the nineteenth century it was rebuilt as a fortified castle by Marchese Nicola Luzzi. Its 6 hectare (15 acre) park is planted with ilex, laurel, pine, elm, linden and very overgrown bamboo. The mature canopy of the trees lends a wonderfully mysterious atmosphere to a series of sculptures, follies and *giocchi d'acqua* or 'water jokes'. Visitors to the park may stumble upon the tomb of the Marchese's wife, a grotto, fragments from classical temples such as columns, broken pediments and amphorae, statues of Pan, a hermit's cell, a gardener's hut or a carousel that really works.

THE GNOME RESERVE, WEST PUTFORD, DEVON, ENGLAND.
A thousand gnomes inhabit the reserve created by Ann Atkin, a grandmother in her sixties who still remembers her days as a hippie art student. Her obsession dates from the 1970s, when gnomes began to appear in her dreams.

The garden is divided into two sections. There is a woodland area which has been cleared to allow dappled light to fall through the leaves onto the gnomes. The majority of the figures are painted and many of them have been made to her specification. They are arranged in groups, some at a tea party, others attending a lecture or a church service. One gnome is lecturing eight green frogs, another group is fishing, some are mining and some are at the seaside. The gnomes are taken under cover each winter and repainted when necessary.

The other area in the garden is a wild meadow intersected by paths. The paths are lined with 250 different species of useful plant, mainly herbs which are identified with labels. Wooden cut-outs of fairies are attached to stakes inserted amongst the plants.

LAMPORT HALL, NORTHAMPTONSHIRE, ENGLAND. Charles Edmund Isham, a Victorian baronet, created a large rockery on his estate at Lamport where he grew miniature plants and dwarf conifers – which were known as 'pygmy fir trees' at that time. Twenty years later he peopled the rockery with porcelain figures that he had bought in Germany.

The Germans call folkloric figures of this kind *gnomen-figuren*. Isham mistranslated this name as 'figures of gnomes', thereby becoming the father of the garden gnome in England.

Isham claimed that his gnomes were supernatural beings. His interest in the supernatural led him to join the Spiritualist Movement. There are records of his reported sightings of 'ghostly miners' and 'several authentic cases of fairies'. Isham was not without humour, however, and he would speculate with friends about what his gnomes might be doing when he was not watching them. His speculations continued for fifty years. The last remaining gnome from those Isham brought to England is now insured for one million pounds.

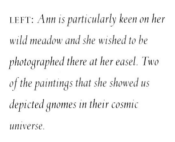

LEFT: *Ann is particularly keen on her wild meadow and she wished to be photographed there at her easel. Two of the paintings that she showed us depicted gnomes in their cosmic universe.*

RIGHT: *This is the last survivor of the German gnomes that Isham brought to Lamport Hall.*

LEFT: *The population of this Belfast garden includes at least sixty gnomes, ladybirds, butterflies, chipmunks, squirrels, swans, frogs and a fox.*

RIGHT: *John Fairnington was not trained as a sculptor. He had not seen any of the animals in real life, and had scarcely ever ventured beyond Whitley Bay. For reference and inspiration, he collected magazine pictures and postcards.*

A GNOME GARDEN, BELFAST, IRELAND. This garden was started eighteen years ago when Mr and Mrs James McCartan and their family moved into their house in Belfast. The very first acquisition was the dolphin and the rest of the collection was built up gradually over the years.

There were eight children in the McCartan family, of whom seven have survived. Most of the plants and ornaments in the garden were presents from the children to their parents. Mrs Joyce McCartan was the proud custodian of the garden until she died three years ago. Since her death the collection has grown rapidly as the McCartan children see the garden as an ever-expanding memorial to their mother.

THE CEMENT MENAGERIE, NORTHUMBERLAND, ENGLAND. Hidden at the back of a semi-detached house in Branxton, a quiet Northumbrian village with a single street, is a garden containing elephants, hippopotami, giraffes, camels, leopards and polar bears. About 300 creatures all compete for space. Life-size, realistically painted but immobile, these creatures are constructed entirely from cement.

This menagerie was the creation of the village's master joiner, John Fairnington. In 1961, at only eighty years old, he started making the animals to amuse his disabled son.

The larger animals, such as a 4 m (14 ft) giraffe, the elephant and the hippopotami were formed *in situ* and anchored to the ground with metal supports. Mr Fairnington was extremely resourceful. The statue of a Hindu riding on a camel and smoking a cheroot contains the false teeth of Fairnington's wife. He worked on until almost the day he died, just short of his ninety-ninth birthday.

LEFT: *Hoarusib the elephant was recreated in bronze by the sulptor David Lomax.*

RIGHT: *The African gorilla Dojum sitting with his grandaughter under a pepper tree. This is the only statue in the garden of an animal in captivity. Dojum lives in John Aspinall's zoo at Port Lympne in England.*

HOARUSIB, BEL AIR, LOS ANGELES, USA. Under a pepper tree in a hillside garden above the Bel Air Country Club is this bronze casting of Hoarusib, a magnificent Namibian bull elephant. His bronze companions in the garden are Torgamba the rhino from Sumatra, Orso the Alaskan grizzly bear and Dojum the gorilla.

John Aspinall is a friend of the garden's owners. He has helped them to locate animals in the wild. Like him, they support the protection of endangered species. Most of the statues are portraits of wild animals. Hoarusib is a local hero in Namibia, because he saved his family from ivory poachers. Sculptor David Lomax filmed him in preparation for modelling and casting the giant beast.

LEFT: *These two willow figures are by Beth Slater. They were part of the 'Mythic Garden' exhibition at Stone Farm.*

STONE FARM, CHAGFORD, DEVON, ENGLAND. June and Kenneth Ashbumer have an extraordinary garden at Stone Farm near Chagford on the edge of Dartmoor, where they have established the National Collection of Alders and Birches. The trees are grown in natural semi-wetland conditions in groves and copses. Each summer they have a sculpture exhibition called 'The Mythic Garden'.

RIGHT: *This stag is by Lynn Kirkham. It is made from long, dried willow twigs woven around a living sapling which provides the stems for the stag's leafy antlers.*

ABOVE: *The figures in the Buddha Park range from life size to monumental.*

THE BUDDHA PARK, WAT KHAEK, NONG KHAI THAILAND. This extraordinary secret grove in north-east Thailand surrounds a temple established in 1978 by the Brahminic yogi-priest-shaman, Luang Pu. He has melded Bhuddist and Hindu mythology, philosophy and iconography into an enigmatic whole. His philosophy has inspired the creation of a series of bizarre cement statues of Shiva, Vishnu, Buddha and a large number of other Buddhist and Hindu deities as well as secular figures.

It is a tradition that anybody who drinks water offered by Luang Pu must turn over all the possessions they are carrying to the temple. Visitors who do not wish to abandon their worldly goods are strongly advised to bring their own drinking water in a canteen, bottle or pilgrim gourd.

SACRED PARK, SOWETO, SOUTH AFRICA. There are thought to be more diamonds two miles beneath the surface of the ground near Soweto than anywhere else in the world. Historically, the diamonds have been owned by a few people with white faces and mined by a lot of people with black faces.

Traditionally the lives of miners have always been short, hard and unpleasant. The Sacred Park was established in the middle of Soweto by the community. It was built to remind the people of their spiritual roots.

A half-life-size dinosaur was constructed in Soweto 63 million years after the species had disappeared from the Earth. Perhaps this was meant to be a way of reminding people that everything is transitory. Not far away was a larger-than-life image of a blue giant called Keva Khayalendaba.

ABOVE: *Keva Khayalendaba — a figure of particular religious importance to the inhabitants of the township.*

LEFT: *Most of the surrounding houses have gone, but the Sacred Park remains. It is well looked after and visitors may still come there in search of inspiration from the blue god and the towering dinosaur.*

KUKS CASTLE, CZECHOSLOVAKIA. In 1662 the estate of Hradiste, north-east of Prague in Bohemia, was bought by a seventeenth-century Czechoslovak soldier who had made a considerable fortune out of the Thirty Years War. His son, Count Frontisek Antonin Spork, transformed his inheritance by building a spa, a hospice and a castle.

The castle was surrounded by splendid baroque gardens. The Count commissioned a Tyrolese sculptor called Matthias Bernard Braun to make a series of allegorical statues of the vices and virtues. However, it is the carvings in living rock on the road to Kuks that are Braun's masterpieces. They are reminiscent of the sixteenth-century carvings commissioned by Prince Orsini at Bomarzo, to the north of Rome.

RIGHT: St John the Baptist, *carved from the living rock on the road approaching Kuks Castle, Czechoslovakia.*

RIGHT: The Vision of Saint
Hubert, *another of Braun's curious
scenes cut from rock.*

THE SHELL GARDEN, SOUTHBOURNE, DORSET, ENGLAND.
Although the creator of this famous and extensive shell garden has
died, it is still visited daily by hundreds of people during the
summer months. George Howard worked in a coal mine in South
Wales from the age of fifteen. Some of his mining equipment is on
display in the garden. After leaving the mines, Howard travelled all
over the world and collected shells and mementoes from many
ports of call. He landed up in Bournemouth in the early 1930s with
seven shillings and sixpence in his pocket. Eventually he began the
shell garden, which he worked on obsessively until his death.

ABOVE: *The Shell Garden is full of
miniature caverns, fountains, seats,
shrines, statues, mottoes and
quotations.*

FIBREGLASS FIGURES, WEST SUSSEX, ENGLAND. Anita Roddick's 4.5 hectare (10 acre) garden is both eccentric and extravagant. Roddick explains her passion for gardening in the following way:

My mother said that when I was forty I would start to love gardens. I live such a busy life that it's either Librium, or Valium, or dope, or gin and tonic or cocaine and, as I don't want any of that, it's my garden that feeds my soul. That's why I don't give a toss about the cost, the garden gives me so much pleasure.

ABOVE: *Roddick favours fibreglass as the material for her fantasies. This fantastic sculpture affords her the pleasure of neighbourly local cows and farmers observing her house every day of the year.*

STANDING STONES, TREVITHICK, CORNWALL, ENGLAND. Edward Prynn lives in Cornwall, the Celtic tip of England. He is obsessed with standing stones, and since 1982 the garden of his bungalow has been the site of his own stone circle.

The stones are granite from a nearby quarry at St Breward. Prynn says, 'I am turned on by rocks and if you run around the stone circle five times, you feel as high as anything, as if you have had a pint of beer'. Occasionally, he goes very far afield for his stones. Two blocks of quartzite came from Mount Pleasant on the Falkland Islands. They were transported 3,000 miles by the contractors that built Stanley Airport.

GIANT WOODEN HANDS, BERKELEY, CALIFORNIA, USA. The 2.5 m (8 ft) wooden hand that is Marcia Donohue's garden gate might be interpreted as a 'halt' sign, but the gate is never locked. The hand provides a charmingly whacky welcome.

The path beyond is made of flagstones carved into the shapes of fallen leaves. It leads into a very personal environment in which Marcia Donohue's sculptures in stone, wood and ceramic are seen alongside Mark Bulwinkle's works in steel. A wild array of sculptural plants provides the setting for this display. The path leads to a view of four Italian cypresses clipped into spirals 6 m (20 ft) high and topped with steel cut-outs of birds. Another giant, wooden hand creates a fence. Its fingers are entwined with roses.

LEFT: *The standing stones are named after important women in Edward Prynn's life — his mother, Marjory, a secret lady, Aunt Hilda, another secret lady, Sally Brown and Jacky.*

RIGHT: *This wooden hand is inscribed with the message 'Secret Egress — An Easy Out' and points the way out of a world of traffic and concrete to somewhere more fanciful, green and quiet.*

FIGWAM, QUEX PARK, KENT, ENGLAND. What appears to be a metal dome or a relic from the Second World War has been placed in a prominent position in the garden of Quex Park and covered with a fig tree, creating a 'figwam'.

GARDEN OF DIVORCE, SAN FRANCISCO, USA. This garden could be interpreted as a symbolic representation of the three themes for which ancient Greek playwrights had an inordinate fondess: sex, money and violence. It was designed by Topher Delaney, one of America's most brilliant and inventive landscape architects. Her approach to private garden design has evolved into what she calls 'the personal narrative'. She finds out what flowers, plants and trees her clients recall from other times in their lives and uses this information to make the garden 'client specific'.

The Garden of Divorce was designed for a client who had suffered a particularly bad separation from her husband. The shattered, jagged pieces of concrete that Delaney placed sculpturally on the slope satisfied the client's post-marital feelings.

RIGHT: *The figwam is a whacky variation on the wigwams of North America. It may have had a practical purpose as the metal 'wam' probably encourages the figs to ripen early.*

BELOW: *The broken concrete slabs in the Garden of Divorce came from a terrace laid by the client's ex-husband. Blood grass is planted amongst the shrubs and trees for symbolic as well as visual effect.*

ABOVE RIGHT: *There are seventeen Davids of two different plaster cast models set alternately around the drive of this Los Angleles house.*

BELOW RIGHT: *At Christmas, the lawn is covered in fake snow. Interspersed between the illuminated statues are silk poinsettias, their petal margins lined with gold paint edging.*

ABOVE: *Misia Sert's semi-precious trees are 35 cm (15 in) tall. Their branches and trunks are made of threaded crystal beads. They are anchored into rock crystal bases decorated with shards of black, pink and red coral.*

JEWELLED BONSAI, PARIS, FRANCE. When Misia Sert died at the age of seventy-eight in 1890, she had been muse to two generations of artists and writers in France. She was immortalized by painters such as Bonnard, Toulouse-Lautrec, Vuillard and Renoir. Poems were written in her honour by Mallarmé; Diaghilev produced ballets, Ravel composed music and Proust and Cocteau transformed her into fictional creatures.

Sert was Russian born and educated in Belgium. She was the wife of two of France's most important and richest publishers before marrying the sensual Spanish painter, Jose-Maria Sert y Badía.

Gabrielle Chanel was one of Sert's best friends. Social historians think that the famous Coco made of mixing real jewels with paste may have been an influence on Sert's exquisite jewelled trees: garniture du table. They were made or, more probably, commissioned by Sert, when she was recovering from her long-time opium addiction after the collapse of her marriage with Sert y Badía.

THE GARDEN OF THE SEVENTEEN DAVIDS, LOS ANGELES, CALIFORNIA, USA. The statues which edge the driveway of this house in Hancock Park are often knocked over or attacked by marauding paint-ball throwers. Perhaps the neighbours are to blame. They probably abhor this garden in their neat suburb of gracious houses, all of them built in that unique Los Angeles *mélange* of styles.

The statues are copies of Michelangelo's *David*, the great and ever-sexy male icon of the Italian Renaissance. A *Venus de Milo* stands alone, surrounded by the youths.

ROSENBLUM MINIATURE TRAIN GARDEN, COLUMBUS, OHIO, USA. Dr Chip Rosenblum and his wife Gail have been creating their train and sculpture garden for the past eighteen years. He is responsible for the trains and she the sculpture. They work on the plants together.

Their initial task was to find plants of the correct scale for a miniature railway. Dwarf conifers, certain annuals and mat-forming species which grow on heavy clay are a boon. They found by trial and error that many of the self-seeding ground cover plants were too prolific. Those described as 'mother-of-thousands' would be better named 'those-that-eat-the-back-yard'. Much of the small-scale hard landscaping material, such as old bricks and gravel for railway track, came from garage and boot sales.

LEFT: *Both of the Rosenblums admit to being obsessed by the miniature train and their sculpture garden. They describe it as a form of therapy.*

6 SURREALISM IN THE GARDEN

Pure psychic automatism which is intended to express... the true function of
thought. Thought dictated in the absence of all control exerted by reason,
and outside all aesthetic and moral considerations.

ANDRE BRETON, *Manifesto of Surrealism* (1924).

T HE TERM *surréaliste* was first coined by Guillaume
Apollinaire, who used it in 1917 in relation to his new
drama *Les Mamelles de Tiresias*. André Breton adopted the
word and defined it in his three Surrealist Manifestos. A task by
which he earned himself the title of 'The Pope of Surrealism'

Among the other artists that contributed to Surrealism were
Max Ernst and Jean Arp, co-founders of the DADAIST movement,
de Chirico, Klee, Magritte and Miró. In 1929, Salvador Dali joined
the Surrealists. His hallucinatory dream images brought the
movement to wide public notice.

RIGHT: *A wonderfully dramatic*
vertical sculpture in Tony Duquette's
Dawnridge garden.

DAWNRIDGE, BEVERLY HILLS, CALIFORNIA, USA. Tony Duquette's career as a famous and highly influential interior decorator was launched in 1943. Now in his eighties, Duquette continues to be a leading influence on international design.

Dawnridge is the name of Duquette's exquisite house in Beverly Hills, where a charming, Regency-style front door belies the magic of the obsessive, eclectic garden kingdom beyond.

Duquette has always been fascinated by the wooden buildings common to Thailand and Indonesia. In the eucalyptus dell in his garden he has built a small Indonesian village. There are nine houses, most of them standing on stilts over the stream. They and linked to the main house by a series of decorative but perilous wooden catwalk bridges.

Tony Duquette also has a refuge in the Malibu mountains called Sortilegium. Sadly, it was burnt down in 1993, but he is recreating

LEFT: Duquette has been brilliantly imaginative in his use of materials. What seem to be exquisite, south-east Asian filigree panels are actually air landing strip sections from a dismantled Los Angeles Navy base.

BELOW: A conservatory salvaged from a Victorian house that was demolished in San Francisco .

its exotic landscaping. He explains his work in the following way:

'I have searched out anything that captured the quality of what I was seeking, whether I found it in the streets, in an attic, out in the desert, or by the sea. I don't like to reproduce whatever exists. I'd rather take a shell, a rock, a tree branch and a grill, and use them to create an angel or a chandelier.'

Duquette has recycled all manner of material, from Hollywood sets to eighteenth-century shop fronts from Dublin.

ABOVE: *High power line insulators brilliantly stacked up as jolly sculptures amongst the agaves. This piece is called* Here Come the Clowns.

RIGHT: *The antlers that decorate this pavilion came from San Simeon, the 'ranch' belonging to Randolph Hearst. Duquette and his late wife were guests there on the final weekend before it was opened to the public.*

THE ENCHANTED FOREST, GROOMBRIDGE PLACE, KENT, ENGLAND. Groombridge Place is a perfect Carolean moated manor house, built in 1664 for a wealthy London merchant. In 1993 it was bought by a business man who has opened the house and gardens to the public.

A small boat on a narrow willow-flanked canal leads from magnificent formal gardens laid out in 1674, to the deep woods where Ivan Hicks has created the Enchanted Forest. For many years Ivan Hicks was head gardener to the Anglo-American millionaire Edward James at Monkton House on the West Dean estate. Now he is the leading British designer of surreal landscapes and gardens.

The owner of the garden is particularly keen that children should be encouraged to explore nature – even though most of the nature they that they encounter at Groombridge Place has been substantially altered by man. Each area of the Enchanted Forest has a sign suggesting what might be found by the inquisitive child. The structures include an enormous spider's web made of sticks, a double spiral and a mystic pool celebrating Celtic tree mythology. Here the perspective is totally distorted by hanging mirrors which revolve in the wind.

RIGHT: *This enormous spider's web leads children up to the branches where Hick's woodland folk, the Groms, have their homes.*

LEFT: *Mirrors hanging from the trees of the Enchanted Forest reflect surreal images of trunks and branches, dappled light and shade, and spooky glintings on the murky pools.*

ABOVE: *The climax of the adventure is the Romany Camp. Here a part-Romany, part-Cherokee lady keeps contact with the outside world by using a cellular telephone.*

PALM GROVE GARDEN, BERMUDA. This relief map of Bermuda is in the garden of the Gibbons family, prominent inhabitants of the island for generations. The map is approached through the garden's moon gate, across impeccable lawns and past aviaries full of toucans and parrots.

RIGHT: *This piece of floating cartography at is divided into carefully manicured sections representing the island's parishes.*

LEFT: *James named some of his structures after the leaders of the Surrealist movement. This is* Homage to Max Ernst.

RIGHT: *The entrance to the Plaza San Eduardo at Las Posas, with a fountain designed by Edward James.*

SURREALISM IN THE GARDEN

GARDEN LAS POSAS, XILITLA, MEXICO. Edward James was one of the great eccentrics of the twentieth century. Both of his Anglo-American parents died when he was relatively young, leaving him extraordinarily wealthy.

During the 1920s and '30s James indulged his passion for painting, poetry, theatre and ballet. He was obsessed by the work of the Surrealists, and he commissioned paintings and sculptures from Magritte, Dali and de Chirico. He was married to Tilly Losch, the dancer, but the marriage ended in a scandalous divorce in 1934. Nevertheless, James commissioned a famous stair carpet patterned with Losch's wet footprints.

After his divorce, James lived only part of the time in England. In 1944 he went to Mexico on a whim. While searching for orchids in the north of the country he found land with a series of exquisite waterfalls. Feeling that he had found his earthly paradise, he bought the land which was near Xilitla. He remained there for forty years, devoting himself to the creation of a collection of surreal structures.

James engaged a young Mexican called Plutarco Gastelum Esquer to be his valet and supervisor of works. They employed sixty-eight carpenters and masons to construct the concrete fantasies in the semi-tropical rain forest. The jobs that they provided supported many families.

The mountains provide a backdrop for the garden at Las Posas. Among the lush vegetation of the rain forest are gates, towers, obelisks, giant snakes, clam shells, lotus blossoms, columns supporting thin air, bridges and spiral staircases leading up and out into space.

Near the end of his life James was still working obsessively on his surreal fantasy garden in Mexico. At this late stage in his life he admitted that he had always possessed too much money, with the result that he had too many choices. In retrospect he thought that he should have been a gardener.

LEFT: *Like so many of James' delicate concrete fantasies, these flowers may soon be overgrown by the rampant foliage of the jungle.*

RIGHT: *These brightly-coloured screens were constructed by James from concrete bamboo shapes.*

ABOVE: *An ornate bridge forms the entrance to James' tower.*

RIGHT: The staircase To Heaven. *James said of his work, 'When archaeologists come and see this in two or three thousand years' time, they won't know what to make of it.' If this tower were to survive, it would certainly pose some questions to future archaeologists.*

LEFT: Five Go Mad at Henley. *Hicks proves time and again that garden sculptures can cost nothing, be witty and lift a garden from the mediocrity of the endless reconstituted stone urns and plinths.*

RIGHT: *This is* Derek, The Green Man. *Hicks allows trees and shrubs to grow more or less as they wish between the sculptural elements, reclaimed bric-à-brac and 'found' objects in the garden.*

THE GARDEN IN MIND, STANSTED PARK, ROWLAND'S CASTLE, HAMPSHIRE, ENGLAND. Ivan Hicks became gardener to Edward James, the great patron and eccentric, at a very early age. Although James lived largely in Mexico, he retained his family home at West Dean in Sussex where he employed Ivan Hicks to design gardens reflecting his passion for Surrealism. The surrealist Garden in Mind, where found objects, sculptures and mirrors are combined with extravagant planting, surrounds Hicks' own house at Stansted Park.

LEFT: *This picture shows three*
different elements of the garden:
Spring Flowers *in the foreground,*
Homage to de Chirico *and the*
surrela gramaphone horn, Catcher.

ABOVE: *Ivan Hicks'* Cosmic Tree
made of cable spools stands on an
earth spiral.

MOSAIC GARDEN, MELBOURNE, AUSTRALIA. Margot Knox is a Melbourne artist who claims at one time to have disliked mosaics. That was before she and her children experimented by covering an old sofa in mosaic. It was at this moment that she began to see possibilities. Knox's previous experience was with working in stone in a Japanese manner. This helped her with her mosaic designs and the garden is now almost enveloped by mosaic interspersed with architectural plants such as agaves and aloes. The plants and the mosaics are encroaching upon each other and eventually there will be no space left at all.

CANNWOOD FARM, SOMERSET, ENGLAND. Polly Devlin and her husband Andrew Garnett have created a garden on the edge of the Salisbury Plain. The design aesthetic is that of the large English garden — with some eccentric differences. Plantings include the secret White Rose Garden and Herb Garden, herbaceous borders, and a new 4 hectare (10 acre) oak wood. Unexpected sculptures have been sited along the paths radiating from the house.

LEFT: *A wall in the Melbourne Mosaic Garden which is visited by hundreds of people every year.*

RIGHT: The Urn at the End of Its Tether *by Shane Barnard, shown in the woods at Canwood farm*

7 ARTISTS' GARDENS

I wanted to give visitors, especially children, a place of Joy, where they could enjoy art and nature together.

NIKI DE SAINT-PHALLE, CAPALBIO, ITALY.

THE ARTISTS IN THIS CHAPTER may have been revolutionary in their time, but they have all found a niche in the art world and a measure of public acclaim. Unlike the majority of artists, they have dared to leave the studio and work on pieces that relate to a wider environment.

PROSPECT COTTAGE, DUNGENESS, KENT, ENGLAND. Derek Jarman's designs for the sets of plays, films and ballet reflect a very individual and quirky visual imagination. In 1986, Jarman bought a wooden hut almost on the beach at Dungeness in Kent. To some, it might appear to be one of the least attractive places imaginable to spend the weekends – it has a nuclear power plant as its closest neighbour. And yet, Jarman's extraordinary imagination was capable of transforming this desolate landscape into a very personal and idiosyncratic garden.

Jarman has died from AIDS, but the garden is still maintained by a group of admirers. Inspired by his life and vision, they have continued to care for it both as a memorial and an inspiration to the casual seaside rambler.

PREVIOUS PAGE: *Jarman combined
sea-washed stone and pebble sculptures
with tough plants such as poppies,
cosmos, sea thrift and sea holly.*

ABOVE: *The garden is filled with
'found' objects, the sea-changed
detritus of the shore.*

CLAUDE AND FRANÇOIS-XAVIER LALANNE, PARIS. The Lalannes were associated with the Neo-Realist school in Paris during the 1960s. They went on to develop their own highly individualistic and brilliant style, working both alone and in collaboration. It has been said that their work echoes the garden sculpture of the eighteenth century, the organic structures of Art Nouveau and even the contemporary theme park.

ABOVE: *The Lalannes are internationally known for their very unusual topiary. They often create metal animals with topiary frame bodies, one such Dimetrodon is also to be found on the Promenade, Santa Monica, California.*

ABOVE: *The Lalanne sheep are triumphs of 'art over nature'. This flock, which has its own sheep-dog to watch over it, was part of a major retrospective in 1998. The exhibition was mounted in the Parc Bagatelle in Paris.*

RIGHT: *These witty tortoises have shells embellished with an intarsia of succulents.*

LEFT: *The front of the Cyclops' head with its single eye. The team like to think that it will be rediscovered after hundreds of years. It amuses them to imagine what future anthropologists might make of it.*

LA TÊTE DU CYCLOPE, FONTAINEBLEAU, FRANCE.
This amazing construction was built in 1970 by Niki de Saint-Phalle and Jean Tinguely, working with Bernhard Luginbuhl, Eva Appeli, Daniel Spoerri, Foknoz and others. The team gave itself the rather impressive title of 'super-collaboration-individual-long-distance-permanent-collective-Gigantoleums-apparat'. The head is some 27 m (85 ft) high. Inside there are spaces designed for theatrical events.

RIGHT: *This is the back of the sculpture. A railway carriage juts out at an angle from one side of the Cyclops' head which is open to visitors from April to October.*

RIGHT: *In the Hamptons the ubiquitous swimming pool is almost always rectangular in shape. During the 1960s Ossorio built this oval pool with a black lining and a red and black asphalt surround. A few of his unusual and rare conifers are visible beyond the pool.*

THE CREEKS, EAST HAMPTON, LONG ISLAND, USA. Alfonso Ossorio made sculptures, paintings and assemblages out of industrial detritus and 'found' objects. In 1951 he bought The Creeks, a 23 hectare (57 acre) estate on Georgica Pond, the forested edge of the most beautiful spot in the Hamptons.

During the 1950s, Ossorio gave parties that were attended by important figures from the contemporary art world. Motherwell, Nevelson, Johns and de Kooning were all regular vistors. Jackson Pollock's fatal car crash occured when he was on his way to a musical evening at the house.

Ossorio became fascinated by his garden during the 1970s and filled it with bizarre evergreen shrubs and trees. He loved conifers with extreme forms, whether they were weeping, contorted or fastigiate. He also liked variegated plants. On one occasion he had three types of spruce grafted together to create one tree with green, blue and yellow foliage.

During this period Ossorrio became so obsessed with unusual plants that he sold off works by Dubuffet, Still and Jackson Pollock to pay for them. On occasions he could spend as much as $300,000 on a single plant order.

LEFT: *The initial inspiration for the Tarot Garden came from Gaudí's Parque Güell in Barcelona, which Niki de Saint-Phalle saw in 1955. She was also inspired by the Sacred Wood of Bomarzo in Italy and Watts Towers, Los Angeles.*

THE TAROT GARDEN, CAPALBIO, ITALY. Niki de Saint-Phalle came to prominence as a sculptor in the 1960s with her large fat ladies, or 'Nanas'. Her most controversial Nana is exhibited in the Moderna Museet, Stockholm. Her body is large enough to be entered through her open legs. Visitors can see a film in one breast and patronize a milk bar in the other.

Since 1979, Niki de Saint-Phalle has been creating her Tarot Garden in Tuscany. In this very private domain, she has encapsulated many of the ideas about sculpture, form and colour that she has been working on for the past forty years.

In all of her work de Saint-Phalle has been influenced by her long-term partner and collaborator, the Swiss kinetic sculptor Jean Tinguely. It is his genius with metal and his overall knowledge of construction that has made the realization of de Saint-Phalle's ideas possible.

In the garden twenty-two of the major arcana of the Tarot are depicted in the form of giant, mirrored and moscaiced sculptures. Although de Saint-Phalle has suffered from uncertain health for a long time, she has chosen to live for many years in the *Empress*, a sculpture in the shape of the Sphinx. Her bedroom is in one breast and the kitchen is in the other.

LEFT: *Visitors can climb inside many of the scultures in the Tarot Garden. Most of them are decorated with mirrors and mosaic.*

ABOVE: *This is* The Empress, *a sculpture representing the Sphinx which serves as Niki de Saint-Phalle's home.*

RIGHT: *Dubuffet's terrace was a tremendously ambitious project. The area at its centre is called the 'Cabinet Logologique'. It is decorated from floor to ceiling with small-scale black, white, red and blue drawings in Dubuffet's unique style.*

BELOW: *This abstract tree rises from the edge of Dubuffet's terrace.*

CLOSERIE FALBALLA, PERIGNY-SUR-YERRES, FRANCE. Jean Dubuffet coined the term 'Art Brut' in 1949. He used it to describe the art of children or the mentally ill, whose work he referred to as the '…purest and crudest… springing solely from its maker's knack of invention and not, as always in cultural art… aping others or changing like a chameleon.' Twenty years later, Dubuffet founded a museum of Art Brut in Lausanne, Switzerland.

In 1970, Dubuffet embarked upon his most ambitious architectural and sculptural project. At Closerie Falballa, his home in Perigny-sur-Yerres, he built a massive terrace from cement and polystryrene. The structure plays upon the ambiguous line between abstract and natural forms.

8 THE ART OF THE SELF-TAUGHT

Nowadays, people are calling me an 'artist'. I don't like this word 'artist', only God pushed me to do this work. I never knew people would see it, I just made it for my own pleasure.

NEK CHAND SAINI.

UNLIKE THE ARTISTS in the previous chapter, these people have never received the recognition of the traditional art world. They create Gardens of Obsession which fall into a quite different category. Here the junk materials cast off by our consumer society are put to good use. Broken plates, glass bottles, car headlights, and scraps of wood all find their place. These gardens are works of art made by the self-taught. They do not fit easily into any of the accepted categories of creation. Perhaps it is significant that the traditional art world should refer to work of this kind as 'Outsider Art'.

PREVIOUS PAGE AND LEFT: *Chris Parsons insists that anyone can create infinite variety of their own images in dew. 'Once you do it, you realize how simple it is. I couldn't walk in a straight line at one time. Then, I took a job with the local council as a groundsman at a public park. That teaches you how to mow in a straight line, I can tell you.'*

BELOW AND RIGHT: *The designs are created on the perfectly smooth turf of a bowling green. Parsons seems quite content with this ephemeral art form.*

THE LAWN ARTIST, BUCKINGHAMSHIRE, ENGLAND. Chris Parsons did go to art school but now he works as a groundsman for a park in Buckinghamshire. He uses a broom to trace magnificent designs in the heavy dews of fine autumn mornings.

Parsons says that October is the ideal month for creating these most evanescent of masterpieces. 'You need a clear night for the dew to form, followed by a clear morning with full sun and no clouds. You brush away the dew in parts, and you're left with design from the sheen of millions of droplets – until the sun gets hot and burns it away.'

PREVIOUS PAGES: *Nik Chand's garden has become the centre for one of the largest recycling programmes in Asia. The armatures for the sculptures are made from old bicycle parts. The forks become legs and the bicycle frames become bodies.*

RIGHT: *These giant rag doll sculptures have unusual rigidity and strength because of their metal armatures and a stuffing made of hundreds of tightly bound rags.*

THE ROCK GARDEN OF NEK CHAND, CHANDIGARH, INDIA. Nek Chand Saini was born in 1924 and moved to Chandigarh in 1948, just at the time that twenty-six villages were being demolished and Le Corbusier was creating a new complex of buildings for the city.

Chand was employed as the Roads Inspector for Chandigarh Public Works Department. He had always been fascinated by strangely shaped stones and when he found himself working in an overgrown area outside the city limits, he started to collect stones and waste material. He brought his finds back on his bicycle to a secret hideaway – his sacred grove.

Chand gradually started to shape his collection into fantasy figures. When the government discovered his sacred grove, there were already 2,000 sculptures in the undergrowth. Nek Chand's creation was illegal and should have been destroyed. It was saved by an enormous public outcry, already many people were fascinated by Chand's work.

Chand was eventually given a salary and fifty people to help him expand his fabulous creation, now known as The Rock Garden. A second phase consisted of a series of courtyards made from natural stone. Chand has continued to expand the Rock Garden and it now covers an area of 20 hectares (50 acres). His self-taught art is internationally recognized and an appeal has been made for an endowment to preserve it. The Rock Garden is second only to the Taj Mahal as the most popular tourist attraction in India.

ABOVE: *The hub-cap fence rows are the first indication that one is approaching the Hub-cap Ranch which lies beyond Napa and St Helena.*

LITTO'S HUB-CAP RANCH, POPE VALLEY, AETNA SPRINGS, CALIFORNIA, USA. In the late 1950s Emanuele 'Litto' Damonte, an Italian immigrant, started decorating his fences, trees, buildings and garden with hub-caps. The first ones fell off as motor cars turned the bend in the road, later his neighbours began to donate them. There are still 3,000 hub-caps on the 25 hectare (62 acre) ranch.

Litto was a stone mason by trade and he worked on William Randolph Hearst's marble pool at San Simeon. Hub-cap Ranch is now recognized by the California State Historical Landmark Commission. Mike Damonte, Litto's grandson, is its curator and he lives on the ranch with his family. He still questions his late grandfather's motives: 'I really don't know what he was trying to do, but then who knew what Picasso was doing?'

THE MUSEUM OF THE WEST, OLD TRAPPER'S LODGE, BURBANK, CALIFORNIA, USA. John Ehn was born of Swedish pioneer parents in 1896. He grew up near Hudson Bay. When he was interviewed during the 1970s, he explained his talent for making statues in the following words:

> There wasn't much to do in that country, so it was natural for us to make things and most people were skilled in one way or another. I don't go for the word talent. Any kind of handiwork is mostly practice and the average workman today could make statues if he had a mind to.

In 1941 Ehn made an open-air museum around his motel in southern California. He took up statue-making in earnest after a heart attack in 1955. In his own words: 'One day I thought to myself, I'm feeling stronger and by golly the time is right, I'll make a statue! I did the best I could, but I wonder why I haven't done it better?'

BELOW: *Sweet Lorraine and Lovely Louise, the concrete saloon girls, taking their ease in John Ehn's museum. The life-size statues are made from sand and cement over an iron core and wire mesh.*

WORLD OF LOST ART, ANDRADE, ARIZONA, USA. Charles Kasling served twenty-four years in the US army and navy. On his retirement he travelled for ten years before settling in Death Valley, California.

Kasling began by making prehistoric animals from cement. After two years he was evicted from the land where he was squatting. He moved on to Andrade, Arizona, where he began to create his World of Lost Art, a group of sculptures made from reinforced concrete. He works by carving the concrete while it is still wet. When interviewed during the 1970s he said: 'If you have a creative mind and can visualize any face or feature of any thing you've got it made. If you have not that ability you might as well throw your trowel away and the cement over the wall and see how it runs'.

THE BOTTLE VILLAGE, SIMI VALLEY, CALIFORNIA, USA. Grandma Prisbrey started to salvage materials from her local dump in 1950. By 1960 she had constructed thirteen buildings out of bottles, televisions, headlights and other detritus. The rooms are stacked with her collections – of which glass, dolls and pencils are just three examples.

Prisbrey was once asked how her garden would change if she had a million dollars. Her reply was characteristic: 'Anyone can do anything with a million dollars...' she said '...just look at Disney. But it takes more than money to make something out of nothing, and look at the fun I have doing it'.

CHICO, CALIFORNIA, USA. Albert Glade emigrated to America from Bremen, in Germany. Over his lifetime he created three gardens. Chico, north of Sacramento, was the last one. Here he assembled pebbles, shells, shards of glass, ceramics and bits of plastic which he fixed in concrete. Mirrors, toys and clear glass sections were set into interior walls, covered walkways and arches. The site was destroyed after Glade's death.

LEFT: *Walls, posts and benches were all decorated in Albert Glade's garden.*

EUFAULA, OKLAHOMA, USA. Irene Gibson Hall was an antique dealer, operating from her own home in the small town of Eufaula, Oklahoma. When her marriage failed, Mrs Hall became obsessed with decorating the outside of her house. She used any materials that she could find – coloured stones and marbles, painted gourds, skulls, plastic flowers and decorated horseshoes. She was also obsessed with dolls and she covered one of the perimeter fences with hundreds of them.

GRAND COULEE, WASHINGTON, USA. Emil Gehrke was obsessed with windmills and whirligigs. He built 850 of them which Vera, his wife, painted and finished. Gehrke made his contraptions from recycled materials. Like so many self-taught artists, he worked for his own pleasure and that of his children, friends and neighbours.

There were 751 pieces of work remaining on Gehrke's death. Some of these were taken as part of an art project at an electric sub-station outside Seattle and others grace the gardens of Disney World, Florida. Another 151 are on permanent display near the Grand Coulee Dam.

ABOVE: *Boots, plastic containers, tea cups, gardening implements, sections of old rubber and plastic hose were all used by Gehrke to make his windmills and whirligigs.*

LEFT: *Irene Gibson Hall in her garden. When she died the site was completely destroyed.*

LEFT: *Marietta Pallis' Byzantine eagle cut from the Norfolk marshes. Her initials are beneath it in the Greek script.*

BELOW: *Marietta Pallis photographed during the summer of 1955. She and her companion Phyllis Riddle are both buried under a block of granite on the eagle's heart. They once used the channels defining the eagle as their swimming pool.*

HOMAGE TO BYZANTIUM, LONG GORES, NORFOLK, ENGLAND.

Marietta Pallis was a rebel and an eccentric. She was educated at Newnham College, Cambridge, even though her Greek father, a wealthy businessman, disapproved, seeing her interest in science and the arts as unladylike. When she took up bicycling, family legend has it that he destroyed her bicycle with his bare hands.

Despite the influence of her father, Pallis pursued her interest in botany, art and travel. When he died in 1935, she bought some land in Norfolk on which she built a small house and studio.

Pallis loved the wild, windswept Norfolk marshland. She is remembered for her vigorous protest against the local water authority's attempt to dredge a waterway in the reed beds. Pallis also felt a need to protest against the Turkish invasion of Chios 500 years ago. She did this by creating an earth sculpture of the double-headed Byzantine eagle and incorporating her initials beneath it. Pallis' great-nephew, Dominic Vlasto, is the steward and guardian of the marshland into which the eagle has been carved.

9 FORMAL GARDENS

Next to the house are four great squares, two on either side of the sayd
long Walke, in the midddst of which are four fine square Fountains, with
four white Alabaster Statues, neatly and artificially cut.

AN EYEWITNESS ACCOUNT *from a 1635 survey of*
Wilton House, Wiltshire.

THE FORMAL GARDEN, beyond all other types of garden, has the most ancient historical and cultural lineage. It is documented in Egyptian tomb paintings, persian paintings and Roman frescoes. There are still Renaissance villa gardens in Italy and gardens in the style of Versailles throughout continental Europe and the United States.

The Medici gardens built around Florence in the late fifteenth century were prototypes for the formal garden. However, it was Bramante's Cortile del Belvedere at the Vatican, designed in 1503, that inspired the gardens of Western Europe for the next two centuries. Today we read endlessly in gardening magazines about the garden 'room'. The idea stems from Bramante's original design for the *giardino segreto* or secret garden, at the top of the double staircase in the Cortile del Belvedere.

Obsessive rivalry between Ippolito d'Este and Alessandro Farnese, two sixteenth-century cardinals, led to the creation of two of the most influential gardens in Europe. The gardens of Villa Caprarola near Viterbo and Villa d'Este at Tivoli served as pattern books for magnificent formal gardens all over Europe.

The whole world knows about Versailles, the most splendid formal palace garden ever created. Duc de Saint-Simon was a courtier to Louis XIV. His attitude to the new gardens at Versailles was extremely ambivalent:

The gardens, which are astonishingly magnificent, but discouraging to use, are in equally bad taste. One cannot reach the freshness of the shade without passing through a torrid zone, at the end of which one has no choice but to climb and then descend a small hill, and here the gardens end. The stone path burns one's feet, but without it, one sinks into the sand and into the blackest dirt. The violence done to nature everywhere disgusts; the abundant waters, forced up and collected again, are green thick and muddy; they shed an unhealthy and perceptible humidity, a smell which is even worse. The whole effect, which one must yet treat with respect, is incomparable, but it is something to admire, and to shun.

Another dark view came from the splendid female diarist Madame de Sévigné. Her report on the early construction of the gardens included details of the numbers of dead workers hauled away from the site in carts after they were poisoned by swamp gases. Nevertheless, Versailles is a lasting memorial to the obsession of Louis XIV and the genius of his landscape architect, André Le Nôtre.

The formal garden had a tremendous revival in the nineteenth century. Newly-affluent industrialists wanted to flaunt their riches. They built grand country houses and palaces in a *mélange* of styles, including the Italian villa, the French château and the Gothic castle. The formal garden was the necessary setting for these houses.

In England, it was not just the *nouveau riche* but also the aristocracy who laid out large and complex gardens. They were extremely labour intensive, but labour was cheap. When a Duchess of Westminster was asked about the number of gardeners at Eaton Hall, she replied that there were *only* eighty-five: fifty-five out in the grounds and thirty under glass.

The formal style continues to be used by twentieth-century designers for it works wonderfully well with modern, rectilinear architecture. Landscape architects who work in this mode design for a small, rich private client base. Their main clients are in the corporate and public sectors. They design formal gardens and landscapes which are orthogonal to the square or rectangular footprint of the building in the still-vibrant 'International Style'.

PREVIOUS PAGE: *The roof garden of the Rockefeller Centre has an entirely impractical and seemingly unused lawn and herbaceous borders edged with obsessively groomed box hedges. The effect is of an idealized English country manor garden.*

ROOF GARDEN. THE ROCKEFELLER CENTRE, NEW YORK CITY.
Some of the citizens of New York may have taken comfort when the Rockefellers chose to build an office complex at the height of the Depression. The Rockefeller Centre is in mid-town Manhattan, opposite St Patrick's Cathedral. Its roof garden, five stories above Fifth Avenue, offers a little serenity in the midst of the frantic hustle and bustle of New York.

It must be pleasant, if somewhat surreal, to have offices overlooking the Rockefeller roof garden, with a view towards the dreaming spires of St Patrick's beyond. The glass and steel skyscrapers towering above Fifth Avenue give the only real clues as to the true location of this grand and whimsical place.

HERRENHAUSEN, HANOVER, GERMANY. This magnificent
baroque garden belonged to the Electors of Hanover. It was laid
out for Sophie, wife of Prince Ernst August, at her summer
residence. The garden has close historical connections with
the English royal family as Sophie was the mother of George I,
who initially needed a translator to communicate with his
English subjects.

A stunning 78 m (250 ft) jet rises from the central pool in a
large, star-shaped 'room'. This is surrounded by smaller, ornate
enclosures furnished with basins, fountains and statuary. Perhaps,
most exciting feature is the green, trapezoid theatre, with its life-
size allegorical statues, completely covered in gold leaf.

BELOW: *The garden at Herrenhausen
is bounded on three sides by a canal.
Large parterres hedged with beech are
divided by a central axis. The two
halves are then further divided into
smaller, hedged compartments, each
with a different ground plan pattern.*

CHENONCEAUX, INDRE-ET-LOIRE, FRANCE. When Henri II succeeded to the throne of France at the age of forty-eight, his lover Diane de Poitiers was already sixty-seven years old. Chenonceaux was Henri's gift to de Poitiers. She ordered the construction of the massive terrace that encloses the garden in 1555. She then set her gardeners the task of transplanting enough wild violets and strawberries from the forest nearby to cover an area of 2,800 m (9,000 ft) The site had been divided into rectangular parterres and these were planted with flowers, vegetables and fruit trees. Lilies and roses were her favourite flowers.

BELOW: *The standard roses that
de Poitiers liked so much have been
replaced by pink and white hibiscus at
Chenonceaux today.*

CHÂTEAU DE FREYR, WAULSORT, BELGIUM. The château is sited on a bank of the River Meuse. The main axis of this French-inspired 7 hectare (15 acre) site is centred on a canal formally divided by pools. Adjacent to the château are the main parterres, which are mirrored in pools of water.

Beyond the parterres lies another pool bounded by four substantial squares of pleached lime. This is the remains of a sixteenth-century design. Additional pools are decorated with oranges in pots, thought to be 300 years old.

BELOW: *The garden of Château de Freyr is completely symmetrical. It has a central axis which spans over 2 km (1 mile)*

CHÂTEAU DE VILLANDRY, TOURS, FRANCE. Dr Joachim Carvallo was responsible for restoring the eighteenth-century gardens of Villandry between 1906 and 1924 – an achievement made possible by his marriage to an American heiress.

The Jardin Potager, or formal vegetable garden, was inspired by Jacques Androuet du Cerceau's sixteenth-century engravings. Du Cerceau's *Les plus excellents bâtiments de France* is in two volumes, written between 1576 and 1579.

The Jardin d'Ornement was designed by the Spanish scholar Lozano. The four compartments planted in box symbolize *l'amour*. The highly complex patterns are based on allegories of love. Hearts, flames and masks, butterflies and fans, swords and dagger blades are all shaped from box.

PUBLIC GARDEN, LISBON, PORTUGAL. Lisbon was rebuilt in the middle of the eighteenth century after a fire and an earthquake. This enormous topiary garden was one aspect of a new, more formal design for the city. It was inspired in part the parterres of Le Nôtre at Versailles, and in part by the Portuguese love of symmetry.

The garden is a ground-level monument which subtly demonstrates the wealth and importance of Lisbon itself and of the Kingdom of Portugal as a whole. It was designed at the time when Portugal was beginning to lose status and power in international affairs.

RIGHT: *Topiary on the scale of this public garden in Lisbon demands a large team of gardeners to maintain it. The hedges must be clipped to a certain height, the decorative elements trimmed, the gravel raked and the seasonal flowers changed as necessary.*

LEFT: *This beautiful photograph of the Jardin Potager at Villandry reminds us of a painting by Mondrian delineated in vegetables.*

ABOVE: *The fretwork pattern of the parterres at Castelgandolfo could have been inspired by the embroidered sleeves of sixteenth-century papal regalia.*

VILLA BARBERINI, CASTELGANDOLFO, ROME, ITALY. The gardens of the Pope's summer residence at Castelgandolfo were renovated between 1929 to 1933. They continue to be maintained to the highest standard.

Adjacent to the villa is the magnificent formal garden. The main parterre is 200 m (220 yds) long. Its box hedges are clipped to a knife edge. The garden gives on to beautiful views of the Campagna immortalized both by Poussin and Claude Lorrain.

STUDLEY ROYAL, RIPON, YORKSHIRE, ENGLAND. Studley Royal was created for Sir John Aislabie, Chancellor of the Exchequer during the reign of Queen Anne. When Aislabie was ruined by the collapse of the South Sea Bubble in 1720, he retired to his Yorkshire estate at Studley Royal, where he worked for twenty years to create the finest water garden in England. On Aislabies's death, his son added the ruins of Fountains Abbey to the estate.

Mr Paul Sykes has meticulously restored the stable block at Studley – a gargantuan task requiring seventeen tonnes of lead on the roof alone. In the early 1990s he commissioned John Sales, chief garden designer for The National Trust, to design an eighteenth-century garden. Latterly, we provided mature yew topiary from Germany, statuary from Italy and tall box cones in Versailles tubs four foot square.

BELOW: *Aislabie commissioned Colen Campbell to build the splendid, quadrangular stable block in 1728.*

Gardens of OBSESSION

RIGHT: *The garden at West Green House contains an abundance of parterres. The uprights of the beautifully clipped topiary create a dge the formal canal hedges.contrast with the ground plan*

BELOW: *In the Rose Garden at Kennerton Green standard tea roses edge the formal canal.*

RIGHT: *A splendid formal parterre roofs the Chardonnay cellar at Newton Vineyard. According to Peter Newton, 'it's a great way to keep the wines cool while ageing'!*

WEST GREEN HOUSE, HARTLEY WITNEY, HAMPSHIRE, ENGLAND. West Green is an exquisite house built in the early eighteenth century. Its superb Queen Anne garden is wonderfully evocative. It contains parterres, a nymphaeum, a green theatre, a lake with a high-arched geometric bridge and a pair of black chinoiserie fruit cages. The property is owned by Marylyn Abbott. Through her energy and vision both the house and the gardens have been completely restored. She has recently created a new topiary garden dedicated to *Alice in Wonderland* .

Many of the garden buildings and ornaments were designed by Quinlan Terry who was commissioned by Sir Alaistair McAlpine, the former owner of the property. Brick walls 300 years old and high hedges enclose the gardens.

KENNERTON GREEN, MITTAGONG, AUSTRALIA. Kennerton Green is another of Marylyn Abbott's gardens. It is made up of a series of mature, inter-connecting areas, each with a single theme. There is a quintessentially English cottage garden laid out around the house, a rose garden a cherry walk, and magnificent shrub and perennial borders. Wisteria grows in abundance. The garden's masterpiece is the wisteria parasol, some 8 m (26 ft) wide.

NEWTON VINEYARD, ST HELENA CALIFORNIA, USA. The Newton Vineyard lies at the northern end of the Napa valley. Its magnificent terraced gardens are the creation of Peter Newton and his wife Su Hua, who draw their inspiration from both Europe and Asia.

BIBLIOGRAPHY

Ardle, Jon, 'Ancient Sagasi' [Japanese *Saga-Giku* chrysanthemums] *The Garden*, November, 1998.

Atkins, Robert, *Art Speak*, Abbeville Publishing Group, New York, 1990.

Atkins, Robert, *Art Spoke*, Abbeville Publishing Group, New York, 1993.

Beardsley, John, *Gardens of Revelation*, Abbeville Publishing Group, New York 1995.

Bermuda Department of Tourism, *Explore Bermuda, History, Culture, Nature*, [Brochure] London, October, 1997.

Bermuda Tourism, *Find Yourself in Bermuda*, [Brochure] London, 1997.

Clarke, Ethne and Wright, George, *English Topiary Gardens*, Weidenfeld & Nicolson Ltd, London, 1988.

Coleby, Nicola (Ed.) *A Surreal Life: Edward James*, The Royal Pavilion, Libraries & Museums, Brighton & Hove in association with Philip Wilson Publishers, London, 1998.

Cornwall, Martin, *The Complete Book of the Gnome: All You'll Ever Need or Want to Know*, AA Publishing, Basingstoke, Hampshire, 1997.

Crawford, Sharon, *Ganna Walska Lotusland, The Garden and its Creators*, Companion Press, California 1996.

Crookshank, Ann, 'Amusement Arcadia', [Larchill] *The World of Interiors*, April 1998.

Elliott, Brent Dr, 'Gnomenclature'. [Garden Gnomes] *The Garden*, April 1992.

Elliott, Brent Dr, *Victorian Gardens*, Batsford, London 1986.

Fieldhouse, Ken, 'Which Way for Worlitz?' [Dessau-Worlitz] *Landscape Design*, October 1997.

For The Friends of Nature and Art - The Garden Kingdom of Prince Franz von Anhalt-Dessau in Age of Enlightenment, Catalogue, Verlag Gerd Hatje, Germany, 1997.

Gallup, Barbara and Reich, Deborah, *The Complete Book of Topiary*, Workman Publishing Company Inc., New York, 1987.

Grounds, Roger, *The Plantfinder's Guide to Ornamental Grasses*, David & Charles, Newton Abbot, Devon, 1998.

Hadfield, Miles, Harling Robert and Highton Leonie, *British Gardeners - A Biographical Dictionary*, Zwemmer Ltd in association with The Condé Nast Publications Ltd, London, 1980.

Hemphill, Herbert W. Jr and Weissman, Julia, *Twentieth-Century American Folk Art and Artists*, E. P. Dutton, New York, 1974.

Hunt, John Dixon, *Garden and Grove*, J. M. Dent & Sons Ltd, London, 1986.

Huxley, Anthony, 'Topiary at Tulcan', *The Garden*, August, 1979.

Jones, Barbara, *Follies and Grottoes*, Constable & Co. Ltd, London, 1979.

Kiester, Edwin Jr, 'Not Your Average Backyard Gardener' [Ganna Walska] *Smithsonian*, March, 1997.

Kingsbury, Noel, 'Charm of The New', [Cannwood] *Country Life*, August 21, 1997.

Lycett Green, Candida and Lawson, Andrew, *Brilliant Gardens*, Chatto & Windus, London, 1989.

Maidment, Barbara, *The Enchanted Forest and Groombridge Place Gardens*, [Guide Book] Blenheim Asset Management Ltd, 1997.

Maizels, John, *Raw Creation: Outsider Art and Beyond*, Phaidon Press Ltd, London, 1996.

Marchesseau, Daniel, *The Lalannes*, Flammarion, France, 1998.

Mazzanti, Anna (Ed.) *Niki de Saint-Phalle - The Tarot Garden*, Edizioni Charta, Milan, 1977.

Miller, Jill Ashley, 'Eccentric to the End' [Lady Mary Coke] *Country Life*, September 1, 1977.

Mott, George and Sample Aall, Sally, *Follies and Pleasure Pavilions*, Pavilion Books in association with The National Trust, London, 1989.

Owen, Jane, 'A Passion for Wildflowers' [Miriam Rothschild] *The Times Weekend*, January 23, 1999.

Owen, Jane, *Eccentric Gardens*, Pavilion Books Ltd, London, 1990.

Owens, Mitchell, 'A Muse with a Vision of Her Own, Built on Crystal'. [Misia Sert's Bejeweled Miniature Trees] *The New York Times*, January 3, 1999.

Plumptre, George, *Garden Ornament*, Thames and Hudson, London, 1989.

Powell, Bill, 'Norfolk's Grecian Turn' [Marietta Pallis' Nature Reserve at Long Gores] *Weekend Telegraph*, May 3, 1997.

Prisbey, Tressa, *Grandma Prisbey's Bottle Village*, Santa Susana, California, 1979.

Reames, Richard and Delbol Barbara, *How to Grow a Chair, The Art of Tree Trunk Topiary*, Arborsmith

Studios, USA, 1995.

Ridgway, Christopher, 'To Walk in a Vision of Economy and Grace' [Oak Spring, Virginia] *Country Life*, January 1, 1998.

Schuyt, Michael and Joost Elffers, *Fantastic Architecture*, Thames and Hudson Ltd, London, 1980.

Strong, Roy and Trevelyan Oman, Julia, *A Celebration of Gardens*, Harper Collins, London, 1991.

Wampler, Jan, Quotes from Charles Kasling in *All Their Own: People and the Places They Build*, John Wiley & Sons, New York, 1977.

Watt, Judith, 'A Bird's Nest in the Chandelier' [Lady Wynne-Jones' Chelsea Garden] Harpers & Queen, March, 1999.

Yinger, Barry R., *The Development of Koten engei*, Thesis, USA, 1983.

Yourcenar, Marguerite (translated by Richard Howard) *The Dark Brain of Piranesi and Other Essays*, Aidan Ellis Publishing Ltd, UK, 1985.

INDEX

ACKNOWLEDGEMENTS:

We would like to thank the following people who have helped in the writing and production of this book:

Marylyn Abbott, Helena Attlee, Elizabeth Braimbridge, Michael Bonfante, Sathaporn Bongkotrana (Rose), Director of Marketing Communications, Hilton International, Bangkok, Kevin Carr, Carlos Caster, Molly Chappellet, Alfred Cochrane, Mary and John Cooper, Topher Delaney, Anne Dewey, Peter Docherty, Tony Duquette, Dr Brent Elliott, Don Feld, Darlena Goetz, Mary Hayley, Ivan Hicks, Jan Hulme, Mark Jackson-Stops, Judy and Hugh Johnson, Konstantin Kirsch, Anne Manson, Research and Administration, Michael Mushak, Ian R. Neale, Martina Nicolls, Simon Nicol: Technodude, Dr Henry Oakeley, James Pierce, Mark Primack, Richard Reames, Charlie Ryrie, Seymour Rosen, Randall Scheiber, Simple, John Ferro Sims, Barbara Sinnott, Nigel Soper, Richard Carl Stange, Paul Sykes, Tim Street-Porter, Blanche and Gordon Taylor, Curtice Taylor, Tom Todd, Rob Tokar, Richard Tracy, Dominic Vlasto, Patricia White, Lorraine Wild, David Williams, Cedric Witt, and Michael Dover, Susan Haynes and David Rowley of Weidenfeld & Nicolson.

PICTURE CREDITS:

Every effort has been made by the publishers and authors to obtain copyright clearance for the photographs reproduced in this book.

Photographs: Heather Angel: pages 22-23, 80; Adrian Baker: page 67; Eric Boman: 146-147; Elizabeth Braimbridge: 21, (top); The Bridgeman Art Library: 28 (top); Collections: 35 (George Wright); Country Life Picture Library: 61 (Clive Borsnell), 140; David & Charles: 76 (top, Neil Campbell-Sharp); Topher Delaney:110, 127; ET Archive: 52, 126, 135; Fondation Dubuffet: 152-153 (all); Ganna Walska Lotusland Foundation: 72-73, 79; Garden Matters and Wildlife Matters Photographic Library: 32-33, 54-55 (Ken Gibson); 111 (both); The Garden Picture Library: 138-139 (John Glover); Harpur Garden Library: 18, 43, 51,109, 133-135; Christopher Hill Photographic Library: 94; The Hutchison Library: 30-31 (Mike Csaky), 100 (Nigel Sitwell), 102 (Nigel Sitwell); Images Colour Library: 34, 176-177, 174-175, 178-179, 180; Images of India Picture Agency: 158-159, 160-161; Mark Jackson-Stops: 46; JFS Library: 49, 92-93, 182; Robert Glenn Ketchum: 78; Konstantin Kirsch: 3, 44-45; Lamport Hall Trust: 93; Andrew Lawson: 47, 48, 56, 57, 58, 63, 64, 65, 68-69, 95, 98, 99, 108, 136, 137 (top and bottom); London Aerial Pictures Library: 170; Norman Y. Lono: 112; Marianne Majerus: 88, 89; Karen T. Massaro: 39; S. & O. Mathews Photography: 24, 26-27; Tony Morrison, South American Pictures: 9, 10-11, 16; New York Film Works: 14-15, 32, 87; Henry Oakeley: 17, 21 (bottom), 74 (both); Chris Parsons: 154-155, 156-157 (all); Clay Perry:107; James Pierce: 162, 164-165; Photobank: 67 (Adrian Baker); Randall Lee Schieber: 6-7, 28, 29 (both); Jim Reynolds: 38, 40 (left); Seymour Rosen: 166-167; 168, 169; Dr Chip Rosenblum: 114-115; Simple, The Roving Garden Artist: 36 (both), 37; Skyscan: 53; Slide File: 54; Stapeley Water Gardens: 76-77 (bottom); Steve Stephens: 182-183; Jessica Strang: 60, 66, 86, 101 (both), 173, 181; Tim Street-Porter: 85, 96, 113 (top), 117, 118. 119, 120, 121; Curtice Taylor: 13, 25, 32, 59, 70-71, 77 (top), 82 (both), 83 (both), 87, 92, 122, 123 (both), 124-125; Gordon Taylor: 41 (bottom), 113 (bottom), 163; Dick Tracy: 185; Dominic Vlasto: 171; Deidi Von Schaewen: 19 (both), 20, 50, 102-103, 104-105, 106-107, 128, 130, 141, 142, 143, 144, 145, 148-149, 150, 151; Wyld Court Rainforest: 75 (Karl Hansen); Barry R. Yinger: 81.